Ancient Greece and Rome

Excerpts taken from:

The World's Story
by Elizabeth O'Neill

Famous Men of Greece
by John H. Haaren

Before Our Nation Began
by Furlong/Sharkey/Sr. Margaret

The Greeks

Gradually the interest of early history moves from Western Asia and Northern Africa, where the two great early civilizations grew up, into Eastern Europe, and we begin to read about people who seem much more like ourselves. This is partly because they belong to the great race of which the English are one branch, viz. the Aryan race, which rolled in over Europe and almost swamped the earlier peoples already on the land. The Aryan race invaded the north of India too, and became the chief people there, as we know from the language still spoken in the north of India. It sounds very different from our own language, but it is quite plainly derived, like it, from the speech used by all the Aryan race before it was dispersed all over the world. Another great branch of the Aryan race was the Persian people, who swooped down upon the lands round the Tigris, the twin river to the Euphrates, and founded a great kingdom there, and then gradually conquered the whole of Western Asia and Egypt. The Persians, however, did not bring new ways into the lands they seized, but were content to learn from the people they conquered. So people went on building and teaching and doing most things in much the same way as they had done before the Persians came.

But in the east of Europe there rose up a great people belonging to the Aryan race who developed a very wonderful civilization of their own. These were the Greeks or Hellenes, as they were called at that time.

While the Jews had been wandering from Mesopotamia into

the Promised Land these people had been pouring from the North into that land which we now call the Balkan Peninsula, and into the islands round about it.

The Greeks were a very wonderful people, clever and beautiful, full of curiosity about men and things. When we first hear about them they were already quite civilized. They lived in towns and built beautiful houses, and very early too they loved and made poetry. The first great poetry that the Greeks made was said to be written by a blind poet called Homer, but

scholars now think that the Homeric poems were written by many men and handed down from one generation to another. They tell of the early days of Greece, and with some history is mixed much that is legend or mere story.

The stories are interesting in themselves and because they show us what the early Greeks thought was great and good. But the stories of Ulysses, of Jason and the Golden Fleece, of the fair Helen and the great wooden horse in which the Greek soldiers hid themselves and so got within the walls of Troy, should be read merely as stories. Later the Greeks wrote plays and poems as great as any which have ever been written. Indeed, it is through Greece that the other countries of Europe have learned many of the best things they know. The climate of Greece was so soft and mild and the country so beautiful that the people were able to live very much out of doors. They were very healthy and happy, and they loved beautiful things. The Greeks tried to bring up all their children to be strong and beautiful, and most of them were so. Being used to seeing only beautiful people their artists and sculptors painted and modelled very fine figures, and some of the statues carved by these old Greek artists remain today among the world's greatest treasures.

The Greeks were very proud of their country and their people. To them the rest of the world were ' barbarians ' or uncivilized. Their patriotism was fired by the religious festivals in which all the Greeks united to do honor to their gods. At first each Greek clan or tribe worshipped together. Each kindled and kept alight a sacred fire in honor of the gods. Never must the fire be allowed to go out under peril of great disaster through the anger of the gods. No barbarian stranger might bring fuel to the fire. The care of it was a sacred trust.

As time went on some shrines became more famous than others, and to the great temples there Greeks from all parts of Greece would go in great numbers. At Delos there was a great shrine, and a still more famous one at Olympia, a beautiful plain in South-Western Greece surrounded by mountains and forming a kind of natural theatre. Here every fourth year the Olympic games were held in honor of Zeus, the greatest of the gods honored by the Greeks. At the Olympic games the best runners from all parts of Greece ran races. Rich men brought their chariots and competed in racing too. Poets brought their offerings of hymns written and sung in honor of the gods. The victors in each contest, those whom the judges thought the best, were crowned before all the people with wreaths of wild olive, while the name of their fathers and the districts from which they came were cried aloud so that the people might do them honor.

Yet, though the Greeks could thus unite for worship and patriotism, they were not all joined together in one kingdom like the English or French today. Each town with the country round it had at first its own government. This was chiefly because the land was broken up by deep bays on the coast and by mountain ranges inland, and it was difficult for the people in one part of the country to travel to another part. So there were many states such as Corinth, Delos, and Thebes, and more famous still than these, Sparta and Athens.

For a time after the Greek people had settled down each state had its king. The first king would probably be the bravest soldier who had led the people to victory in war, but when he died his son would become king, and then his grandson, and in time some of the kings were not brave men at all, and nearly everywhere in Greece the people said they would not have kings any longer, but chose several of the greatest men in the land to rule them instead. Government by a few great men was called by the Greeks an 'aristocracy.' Generally in time the states grew tired of the aristocracies too, if they became proud and selfish, and in most Greek states some one man seized power again. He was not a king, but was called a ' tyrant,' which did not mean a cruel and selfish person as it does now. Soon again in nearly every Greek state the tyrants were overthrown, and some states chose once more to be governed by an aristocracy.

Sparta chose thus, and was so governed as long as she remained a state. But some of the states declared that all the people should have a share in the government, and these were called democracies.

The greatest of these was the state of Athens, whose people were perhaps the bravest and most beautiful, and certainly the cleverest in the whole of Greece. Athens was the most beautiful of all the Greek city-states. Every one of its people was educated, and every man had a vote and took a direct part in the government. The state was so small that all the men could meet together to choose their leader. It was a very vivid eager life which the Athenians led, all keenly interested in politics, in philosophy and in artistic things. In Athens, every Greek had time and opportunity to hear beautiful poetry, to see good plays acted in theatres open to the air. All took an interest in the building of temples and in the beautiful statues made to adorn them. Perhaps no nation in history has ever had so fine a people, so little poverty, and so much education. But it must be remembered that in Athens, as everywhere in Greece, there were many slaves, who did the hardest work, and so made possible the brighter lives of their masters. The Greek 'democracy ' was not like the modern democracy which most people think is the best form of government. The Greeks did not consider the welfare of all the people, and in modern nations where all are free the problem of making all happy and comfortable is more difficult.

The Spartans

Sparta, the other great city-state in the south of Greece, was not a democracy, but remained an aristocracy. Its people were sterner and not so bright perhaps as the Athenians. They believed that every man should be a soldier, and every boy was taken from his mother when he was seven years old and brought up with other boys and taught how to fight. A Spartan boy would never cry whatever happened. He never thought about being warm and comfortable, but wore the same clothes summer and winter and cared only to be strong and brave. This was the ideal of the Spartans, the thing they lived for. The women felt just the same as the men about it, and the mothers gave up their boys willingly for the sake of the state. The girls shared the games and races with the boys, and grew up strong and brave women. A mother would much rather that her son should die in battle than give in. ' Return with your shield or upon it,' she would say as her son went forth to battle.

Besides the Greeks in the Balkan Peninsula and in the islands round about it there were others who had gone forth across the sea and built cities on the coast west of the land now called Asia Minor.

Since the Phoenicians had led the way men knew much more about ships and how to sail the seas safely, and some of the more adventurous Greeks had sailed westwards and set up towns in Sicily and in the south of Italy. Some of these were very rich and beautiful. The towns on the coast of Asia Minor, too, flourished and grew rich, and were full of beautiful temples, for the Greeks during many hundreds of years worshipped many gods. It was a long time before their cleverest men realized that there could be only one God, and then the people were very angry with them for saying so. Meanwhile, they built their temples to Apollo the god of beauty, or to Diana the goddess, whom they pictured as a huntress, young, brave, and noble, armed with bow and arrow, and with fluttering graceful garments short to the knees. There was one famous temple of Diana at Ephesus, one of the chief Greek towns in Asia Minor. We read in the Bible how in later days St. Paul tried to teach the Ephesians about our Lord, and how they clung to the worship of their goddess. But long before this a great danger had threatened Ephesus and the other Greek settlements in Asia Minor, a danger which threatened Greece, too, and which was so great that in the end the Greeks joined together to resist it.

The Persians

For hundreds of years the Greek towns in Asia Minor, like those at home in Greece, and the colonies in Sicily and the south of Italy, were prosperous and free, but at length they fell under the power of the Lydians, a people who possessed the land near. The Lydian king, Croesus, had conquered most of Asia Minor, and had demanded tribute of the Greek cities there. Croesus was wonderfully powerful and rich, but he fell in his turn before the Persian power, which had now spread westward over Babylonia and on to the very coast. When, last of all, the Greek cities there were attacked by this great barbaric power, they sent distressful messages to their kinsmen in Greece proper, and Athens determined to send them help.

This decision of the Athenian people is one of the turning-points in the world's history. If Athens had not fought against Persia and won, the Persian power might have spread from Asia to Europe, and the whole history of the world would have been changed. The Persians belonged to the Aryan people, but they were quite unlike the Aryan people in Europe. They were brave men, but they had no idea of the freedom which was the ideal of the Greeks. With the Persians, as with most Eastern people before and since, the will of the king was the supreme law. On his word depended life and death. The greatest nobles bowed before him as though he had been a god. His court was full of beautiful things, and life seemed gay and brilliant, but there was a sense of uneasiness, for under a cruel or capricious king no man could feel that even his life was safe.

A story is told of the cruelty of one of these early kings. A nobleman had offended him, but the king pretended to forgive him and invited him to a feast. At the end of the meal the king asked him what he thought of the food, and when he had been assured that it was excellent, the king called for a basket and showed it to his guest. In it were the head, hands, and feet of the nobleman's own child, and the king maliciously told him that the food that he had eaten was his child's body.

The poor people were very poor and often unhappy. Women were hardly thought of as human beings, and children could be sold by their parents as slaves. The 'Great King' could lead great armies to battle, but the soldiers did not feel that they were fighting for their fatherands. They won because of their great numbers, and because they were often fighting men very like themselves. But things turned out very differently when the Persians found themselves fighting with the Greeks, men who loved freedom and beauty and goodness, men who were full of pride in their people and respect for themselves.

When Croesus was conquered by the Persian king, Cyrus, the Greek cities had been forced to give in to him too. Instead of the mere tribute that they had paid to Croesus, they were placed under Persian governors and treated as a conquered people. One town, Miletus, was allowed some sort of independence, but even there the people never felt really safe. The tyrant of Miletus had been carried off into honorable captivity with the Persian king, but had left his son-in-law, Aristagoras, to govern Miletus. The rulers of the other cities had become mere servants of Persia, and so the people determined to get rid of them and set up democratic governments. This they did. Aristagoras took the lead in the movement, gave up his power into the hands of the people, and when, in the year 500 B.C., the Greek cities of Asia Minor announced that they would no longer live under Persian rule, it was Aristagoras who went over to Greece proper to ask help of the Greeks there for their kinsmen over the sea. He went first to Sparta, and told them first of the sad state of the Greeks in Asia Minor, and then of the riches of the Persians. It would be easy, he said, to conquer the Persians, barbarians who wore trousers and turbans, and then all the wealth of Persia would be theirs. But the Spartans refused to go.

Then Aristagoras went on to Athens, and again told his tale. The Athenians had but lately got rid of their tyrants. They were full of spirits and courage. Aristagoras reminded them that Miletus, the chief town suffering under the Persians, had been founded by people from Athens. The Athenians determined to give them help, and sent twenty ships across the seas. The Lydian town of Sardis was accidentally burnt, and the Athenians, without giving further help, went back to their ships, and so home. It was after- wards said that the new Persian king, Darius, was so angry with the Athenians that he told one of his servants to remind him before every meal of the vengeance he was to take on them. But it was eleven years before Darius tried to revenge himself on the Athenians. Meanwhile he turned his anger against Miletus and the other rebel cities. Miletus was taken, and many of its men were killed. The others were sent with the women and children to a town far away on the river Tigris, and there had to live out their lives as exiles far from home and country. The other rebellious cities were badly treated too, and then, after eleven years, Darius turned to take vengeance on the Athenians who had dared to defy him. He sent messengers to Greece asking the states to send him earth and water, as a sign that they would consent to live under the yoke of the 'Great King,' as he called himself.

The Battle of Marathon

Some of the states did so, but Athens and Sparta proudly refused ; and it is said that Sparta threw the Persian messengers into a pit, and told them to find earth and water for themselves there. In the same year, 490 B.C., Darius prepared a great fleet of ships, filled them with soldiers, and sent them against the Athenians. Thousands and thousands of them clothed in mail poured from the ships into the plain of Marathon, which was twenty miles from Athens and belonged to it. The Athenians sent for help to Sparta, but were told that no help could be sent until after a religious festival, which was still some days off*. The Spartans were never very ready to join with the Athenians, for the two states were very jealous of each other. It is said that Pheippides, the runner chosen to carry the message to Sparta, ran all the way in two days. The distance was one hundred and fifty miles.

When he came back the Athenians stood on the mountains looking down upon the plain of Marathon, and the generals consulted together as to what should be done. Miltiades, one of the generals, advised an immediate attack, and the others gave up their power to him, and he arranged the battle according to his will. The Athenians by his orders plunged down from the mountains on to the Persian army in the plain. There were five times as many Persians as Greeks, but the shock was so great, and the Athenians fought so well, that the great awkward army of men, who had no knowledge of what freedom meant, were driven into the sea and back to their ships by the splendid Greek soldiers.

The Greeks clung on to the Persian ships, meaning to set fire to them, but the Persians slashed savagely at them. The brother of Aeschylus, the great poet and writer of plays, who also fought at Marathon, had his hands cut off as he clung to a ship, and then he held away. The Persians sailed round to attack the harbor of Athens next morning, but the Greek soldiers, weary as they were from the battle, marched to meet them, and when the Persians saw the men who had just conquered them drawn up again to face them, they gave up the attack and sailed away in disgust.

So Athens saved Greece, and probably Europe; for Darius, if he had conquered Greece, might have spread his empire over the whole of Europe, and the ideas of freedom and art and beauty which the Greeks taught the world might have been lost. The Athenians built a great monument on the plain of Marathon to commemorate their victory, and they made the men of the little town of Plataea citizens of Athens. Plataea alone of the Greek states had helped the Athenians, and the thousand men whom they had sent were among the bravest and best fighters in the great battle.

Miltiades, the victorious general, soon fell into disgrace. He asked the Athenians to ht out for him a fleet of ships, but begged them to allow him to keep as a secret the purpose for which he wanted them, promising to bring a great deal of money back. Then he sailed away to fight an enemy of his own who lived in Paros, an island near. He was not able to take the city, and sailed back again to Athens without having done anything and without the money he had promised. The

Athenians were very angry, and Miltiades would have been put to death but for the memory of his courage and cleverness at Marathon. He was ordered to pay a fine of a large sum of money, but died before he had time to do so. Some people have blamed the Athenians for having been so severe against a man who had done so much for them, and they have said that people governed as democracies are always changeable. Still, Miltiades had no right to use his country's money to take revenge on his own enemies.

Yet the Athenians were perhaps a little changeable, for they showed it in their treatment of others. The two chief men in Athens after Marathon were Themistocles and Aristides. Themistocles was anxious that the Athenians should build a fleet, and so be able to fight on sea as well as on land, while Aristides would have preferred a policy of peace. In the end Themistocles got his way and Aristides was banished, for the Athenians had a custom of sending troublesome politicians into exile, so that they should not hamper the rulers at home. When the votes were being given as to whether Aristides should go or stay, one man at least was said to have voted against him because he was tired of hearing him called Aristides the Just.' Aristides was not long away, for Persia soon threatened again, and Athens was glad to call back all the exiles who had been sent away after Marathon. (*The full story of Themistocles and Aristides can be found on page 72 and 76.*)

The Persian Invasion of Greece

Darius went back to Persia determined to prepare a monster

invasion of Greece and so take his revenge, but he died before he had time to carry it out, and the work was left for his son Xerxes, who became king after him.

Xerxes invaded Greece in the year 480 B.C. He had endless resources at his disposal in men and money. Fearing the stormy sea round the Cape of Mount Athos, which his fleet would have to pass on its way to the Greek peninsula, he ordered great gangs of men to cut a deep channel through it, so that two ships could easily sail through side by side. Then he ordered bridges of boats to be made across the Hellespont, and in the towns, all along the way by which his army would have to go, he stored great quantities of food. He meant to avoid all risk. The

first bridge broke because the ropes were not strong enough, and Xerxes ordered that the men who had built it should be beheaded. In his mad anger he ordered, too, that the water of the Hellespont should be whipped with rods, receiving three hundred lashes for its defiance of the Great King.

Then the bridges were built again with stronger bonds, and in a fit of repentance or amiability Xerxes poured wine from a golden bowl into the Hellespont, and then flung the cup and a golden bowl and a sword into the water, at sunrise of the day when he was at length ready to lead his great unwieldy army into Greece. The baggage, with the camels and horses, crossed on one bridge and the soldiers on the other. The first to cross were ten thousand Persians, the flower of the army, brave strong men accustomed to conquer. Behind them went the sacred horses and a chariot, empty in honor of the gods, and Xerxes himself drove after. Behind him straggled an enormous host, to the number of at least a million men, drawn from the peoples conquered by the Persians, and with no heart for the fight. So great was the crowd that the two bridges were filled with men and animals crossing over during seven days and seven nights.

It is said that one old man who had sent four sons to the army begged that the fifth might stay at home, but Xerxes, instead of granting the favor, ordered that the boy should be killed, and the pieces of his body placed on both sides of the bridge as a warning to others who might wish to hang back. Any who were slow to cross were freely lashed with whips. Xerxes could not realize that fear will never lead an army to victory.

When the Greeks had seen the danger threatening from Persia, some of the states had been very anxious that the whole of Greece should join to resist it. A congress of the states was called to meet at the Isthmus of Corinth. The part of Greece south of the isthmus was called the Peloponnesus, and here Sparta was the chief state, and had great power over the others. So nearly all the Peloponnesians naturally joined with Sparta, though Argos, a Peloponnesian town, held aloof, declaring she would rather be ruled by the Persians than help Sparta, whom she hated. In the end very few of the states north of the Isthmus of Corinth joined in the defense. There was, of course, Athens and the people of Phocis, and the faithful little town of Plataea, and Thespiae, another town near. But most of the northern Greeks held aloof, and some hastened to send earth and water to the Great King. Themistocles had his fleet ready, and was longing for a good sea fight, but as Sparta was the chief state in all Greece for the moment, the chief command was given to them both by land and sea.

The Story of Thermopylae

As ranges of mountains stretch across the north of Greece, the Greeks knew that the Persian army must come through mountain passes. They decided to make a stand at the Pass of Thermopylae, for if the Persians could get through that, there would be nothing to stop them until they reached the Isthmus of Corinth. A band of men were therefore set under the Spartan king, Leonidas, to guard the pass. More Spartans were to be sent later when a feast should be over. The Spartans would never let anything interfere with their sacred feasts. However, Leonidas knew that a few men could hold the pass easily against even the immense army of Xerxes, but unfortunately a treacherous Greek went to Xerxes and told him that to the west of the Pass of Thermopylae was a path over a mountain which could not easily be defended. Leonidas had placed some Phocians there, but when they saw vast numbers of Persians advancing they turned and fled.

News came to Leonidas that the Persians were advancing, and he knew that there was no hope for those who should remain to guard the pass now that it would be attacked from both ends. So he told his army that those who wished might go away, but that he himself would stay and die fighting the enemy. Three hundred Spartan soldiers with their slaves, and seven hundred others chose to stay, only about a thousand men in all. The Spartans were never afraid, not even of death, and they spent their time making an elaborate toilet, combing out their thick hair, which they wore long, putting on dresses of bright scarlet, and polishing their weapons, so that they might face death with every sign of joy.

As the Persians poured into the plain south of the pass, Leonidas told his men to fight their way out of the northern end ; and there he and his little band died fighting desperately, killing far more Persians than their own numbers. The Persians were astounded at such courage, and angry too that so many of their own men were killed by a mere handful of Greeks. Two brothers of the Great King himself were among the dead. Later the Greeks built monuments on the spot where the heroes of Thermopylae had fought, and chief among them was a marble lion to honor the memory of Leonidas.

In spite of the heroism of Leonidas and his Spartans all Greece, as far as the Isthmus of Corinth, now lay open to the

Persians, and as they marched south the states gave in their allegiance. Plataea and Thespiae were beaten down to the ground, and the Athenians, seeing that there was no hope for them, took refuge on the fleet, and were carried off to Salamis and other places of safety. One of the oracles had advised them to trust to a wooden wall, and this they thought meant their wooden boats; but a few men remained behind in the Acropolis, the hill center of the town, which could not be entered when the gates were shut except at one side. Across this side the Athenians who remained placed great beams of wood to form a kind of wall, hoping thus to fulfil the words of the oracle, and take shelter behind a wooden wall. When the Persians advanced to attack them they threw great stones down on their heads. But it was of no use, for the Persians broke through the barrier, killed the Greeks, and practically destroyed Athens.

Thus the fate of the Greeks on land was sad enough, in spite of their great courage; but there was still the fleet, in which Themistocles had put so much trust. The Persian fleet, off the coast near Thermopylae, had suffered much from storms, and in a fight they had with the Greeks, though the Greeks lost some ships, the Persians lost more. When the news came of the destruction of Athens the Greek fleet was at Salamis. Themistocles could not persuade the leaders to sail forth and attack the Persians. One of the generals said to Themistocles, 'O Themistocles, those who stand up in the game too soon are whipped' (referring to a rule in the Greek games); but Themistocles answered, 'Yes, but those who start late are not crowned.'

At length Themistocles had recourse to a trick. He sent word to the Persians that the Greek fleet was very frightened, and was going to sail away. The Persians then thought it would be best to attack the Greeks before they could escape, and one morning the Greek fleet found the whole Persian fleet drawn up to the east, ready to fight.

The Greeks then showed that they could fight on sea as well as on land, in spite of their hesitation. They dashed in and broke the front line of the Persian ships, and drove the two back lines in confusion upon each other. On sea, as on land, the Persian forces were too awkward and unwieldy. There was really not room for so many ships. The battle became fast and furious. When a Persian ship was sunk the men were drowned, for few of them could swim; while many Greeks even from ships which were destroyed saved themselves by swimming to the shore.

Xerxes had one ally who was a woman, Queen Artemisia of Halicarnassus in Caria. The Greeks had promised a prize to whomsoever should capture her; but when a Greek ship was chasing her she willfully sank a Persian ship which came in her way. The Greek captain seeing this, and not knowing it was Artemisia's ship, gave up the chase, thinking that she had deserted from the Persians.

Xerxes sat on a great white marble throne on the shore and watched the battle. Even at the end the Persians had twice as many ships as the Greeks, but so many men and ships had been destroyed that they had no longer any heart for the fight. Orders were given that the fleet should sail away; and Xerxes himself, sick at heart with disappointment, collected what remained of his vast army, and crossed the Hellespont in haste, lest the Greek fleet should come to stop him. Three hundred thousand Persians remained in Greece under the general Mardonius to make one more attempt in the next year at the conquest of this small country, which had thus defied the giant armies of the Great King.

Xerxes met with endless misfortunes on the journey home. The bridges across the Hellespont broke; the ice gave way on a frozen river as the army crossed it; provisions ran short and disease broke out. Men and animals died in thousands. Mardonius spent the winter in Thessaly, and in the spring started again towards Athens. Once more the Athenians withdrew to Salamis, and their city was again ravaged by the enemy. The Athenians sent indignant messages to the Spartans, who had again failed to help them, because their religious festivals held them back. Meanwhile they had built a strong wall across the Isthmus of Corinth. It is said that someone pointed out to them that the Athenians might in the end join the Persians against Sparta, and that their strong wall would be of little use if the Athenians with their magnificent fleet attacked them by sea.

At last the Spartans sent an army to join the Athenians, and Mardonius withdrew north into Boeotia, which was better country for his cavalry to fight in. Help from other Greek states now poured in, and Mardonius, anxious to break up the Greek army, sent Masistios, the commander second to himself, to attack Megara. The Athenians detached themselves from the general army and went to their aid. Masistios was a handsome man, and almost a giant in height. He wore a suit of golden mail, and over it a tunic of crimson. His white horse was shot under him, and though his mail resisted all arrows for a time, he was at last shot through the eye and killed. The Athenians won the victory, and the body of Masistios was carried in triumph along the lines of the Greek army that all might see it.

Mardonius waited several days before he ventured to attack the Greeks, and then one day, when the Spartans were making a change in their position, he led his army against them alone. The Athenians were surrounded by the Greeks, who were helping the Persians, and so the Spartans fought the famous battle of Plataea practically alone against the Persians. The splendid Persian cavalry tried to break the solid mass of the Spartan ranks, but failed. The heavily armed and mailed foot soldiers of Sparta broke down the hedge of shields, behind which the light-armed foot soldiers of the Persian army stood; and though it was a hard -fought battle, and the Persians were overwhelmingly greater in numbers than the Spartans, the splendid discipline of the Greeks won the day. Mardonius himself was killed, and the Persians fell back to their camp. Here another struggle took place; but the Athenians now came up to the help of the Spartans, and the Greek victory was complete.

All the precious vessels of gold and silver which Xerxes had been too hurried to take away, and so had left to his officers, now fell to the Greeks, and in some degree repaid them for the immense expenses of the war. It is said that only three thousand Persians were left alive out of the three hundred thousand of Mardonius' great army, while in all only one hundred and sixty

Greeks died on the field.

On the afternoon of the day in which the battle of Plataea was fought in the morning, the Greeks won another great victory over the Persians at Mycale in Asia Minor. Here it was the Athenians who played the chief part, going to the help of the Greek cities in Asia Minor, who were still under the hated rule of the Great King. The Persian admiral drew up his boats on the shore, but the Athenians followed, landed, and fought against them on land, and won a great victory. So not only were the Persians driven out of Greece proper, and Europe saved from an invasion by an Eastern people, but the Greeks in Asia Minor were freed from their rule ; and soon they were to be followed into their own strongholds, and the magnificence of the Great King was to be a thing of the past.

The Athens of Pericles and Socrates

Athens had very nobly allowed the Spartans to take the lead in the great struggle with Persia, but once the danger was past the old jealousy between the two states broke out again. Pausanias, the Spartan leader, who had fought so bravely and won so glorious a victory at Plataea, soon proved himself unworthy of the position he held, and Athens took advantage of this to place an Athenian at the head of her fleet. Pausanias was found to be writing to the Persians, and even planning to give Greece up into the power of the Great King, if he himself should be allowed to marry the king's daughter, and if all sorts of riches were showered upon him.

When the Spartans sent messages to the Persians through Pausanias it was noticed that no answer ever came, and so a slave who was given a letter to take, opened it to see what it said. He found that it merely told the Persians to kill the messenger (himself). The slave took the letter to the judges at Sparta, and Pausanias, who had already been called back to Sparta, was condemned to death. He fled for shelter to the Temple of Athene; and as it was not considered right to kill a man in so holy a place, or even violently to drag him forth, the Spartans ordered that the doors of the temple should be blocked up, and the roof taken off so that Pausanias soon died a miserable death through cold and hunger.

Meanwhile the Athenians had built very strong walls round their city and round their port at the Piraeus. Now with such strong walls and their mighty fleet they had no need to fear anybody, and the Spartans were surprised and angry to find that the new leader they sent to Athens in place of Pausanias was sent back with the message that the Athenians had chosen a leader of their own.

After this there was a terrible enmity between Sparta and Athens. Athens was now quite equal in wealth and importance to Sparta, and she took steps to make herself still richer and more powerful. She kept up an immense navy, and many of the islands in the Aegean Sea, Thrace, and some of the Greek colonies in Asia Minor joined in a league with Athens. They were all to send ships and sailors, and all to defend each other against any enemy. The League was called the Confederacy of Delos, and all the money belonging to it was kept at the Temple of Apollo at Delos, and each state sent men there to worship the god. But in time Athens often allowed the other states to send money instead of ships; and after a while she forgot that the other states had joined her of their own free will, and she began to think herself the chief state of a sort of empire, with the other states paying tribute to her. In the end this was very bad for Athens, for it made the other states angry and ready to help her enemies against her.

But this was not for a long time yet, and for many years Athens grew richer and richer. She kept up an immense navy; but there was more money than was needed for that, and some of this was spent on raising beautiful buildings in Athens and making life very easy for her people. Even the men who met in their parliament to rule the state were paid for their time and trouble. The Athenians became great traders, and sent their merchant-ships to all parts of Greece. Gold and silver were quite common.

But the Athenians were not like the Persians, who wasted their wealth on mere splendor and show. Nor had they any sympathy with the Spartans, who, however rich they might be, would never change from their plain, hard way of living. The Athenians loved beautiful things, and they spent their money in making their city perfect and in giving joy and pleasure to all the citizens.

Pericles

The chief man in democratic Athens for many years after the Persian Wars was Pericles, one of the most famous men who have ever lived. He never trusted Sparta, and knew that a great struggle with that state must come some day. He was made 'general' of the Athenian people; but he was always careful to remember that he held power from the people, who chose him to rule as their best and wisest citizen. Unlike so many of even the bravest Greeks, he was faithful and honest in small things as well as great. He was kind, too, and on his deathbed, when the men round him were talking of the great and noble things he had done, he reminded them that he was to be praised not for these things, but because he had never caused sorrow to a fellow-citizen. This was remarkable at a time when the Greeks were terribly cruel and revengeful to anyone who offended them.

Yet Pericles had done wonderful things, for which his fellow-citizens might justly praise him. It was said that 'he found Athens of brick and left it of marble.' The whole city had practically to be built again after the Persian attack. A giant statue of the Goddess Athene made of bronze was made and placed on the highest point of the Acropolis. Then the Athenians planned and built the Parthenon, a beautiful temple of marble, the ruins of which remain to-day to show men how beautiful the buildings of Greece could be.

Right round the outside of the temple ran a frieze or band of sculpture, carved by Phidias, perhaps the greatest sculptor who has ever lived, and by his pupils. Bits of this frieze have since been carried off by other nations. Some may be seen in the British Museum in London, and others in the Museum of the Louvre in Paris. They are considered among our greatest treasures of art. Inside the temple was another immense figure of Athene, carved by Phidias himself from ivory and gold, as marble was not considered rich enough. The great public buildings were adorned with pictures telling of the legends of early Greece and of the wars of later times. A great theatre, too, was built. It was a fine building-, and had no roof, so that the Athenians with their fine climate could see plays acted in perfect comfort.

Just as the age of Pericles was the time when the greatest artists of Athens lived, so, too, it was the age of the great Athenian play- writers. It seemed as though the joy of victory over the Persians had spread through the nation and inspired the cleverest men in the most wonderful way. This kind of thing has often been noticed in the history of nations. A nation will grow strong and fight for its freedom, and it will be found that the age of great soldiers will be also the age of great poets.

The first of the great play-writers of Greece was Aeschylus, and he fought with all his strength at Marathon. In the age of Pericles lived two other great tragic play-writers, Sophocles and Euripides, and their plays, which students read today with the greatest admiration, were then played before the Athenian people in their beautiful open-air theatre; and the people wept over them and gained new ideas from them, and went away full of joy and wonder at

the beautiful things they had seen and heard. Sophocles had been a boy, of sixteen at the time of the battle of Salamis, and he was chosen, because he was so beautiful and could play so well on the lyre, to lead the chorus of boys who took part in the thanksgiving ceremonies on the island of Salamis to celebrate the victory. Then, too, there was Aristophanes, a writer of comedies which made people laugh instead of weep. (*For more of the story of Pericles, see page 80.*)

Socrates

The age of Pericles was the time, too, when the great Greek thinkers and philosophers gave their teaching to the world. The first great Greek philosopher was Socrates. The most educated of the Greeks had begun to ask questions about the real meaning of the world and the things around them, but Socrates was the first who gave any real answer. He understood that the tales about the gods of Greece and of the other nations could not be true, and that there could only be one God. He might have been seen any day in the streets of Athens asking questions of boys and young men, who crowded round him to listen to his wise answers. When they gave foolish or thoughtless answers he laughed, and showed how necessary it is to think before we speak.

Socrates was a little ugly man with a flat, snub nose, but he was a very noble character. He would talk to any man he met, workmen as well as scholars, and he longed to help men to be good and truthful. He loved the town with its crowds and liveliness, and many of the people loved him. He dressed always in the poorest clothes and ate the simplest food, for he thought that these things did not matter. He cared only for knowledge and goodness. In the end he had a very sad death.

Some of the people at whom he had laughed were very angry with him. Others thought that it was very dangerous that their young men should be told that the old tales about the gods were not true. After the death of Pericles the Athenians, spoilt by success, had grown very changeable and restless. Socrates irritated them by insisting that goodness consisted in doing right, and that offerings to the gods were of no use without this. Thirty years after the death of Pericles, Socrates, now seventy years of age, was called before the judges, and put on trial for offences against the gods and the state. He was condemned to die, but did not seem in the least afraid. He even vexed the judges by joking on the subject. When they asked him to suggest what else the Athenians might do to him instead of putting him to death, he suggested that they should keep him in a certain hall in Athens, where men who had served the state were kept at the expense of the state. The judges indignantly passed sentence of death on the old philosopher, and he spent some time in prison before the time appointed for his death.

One of his followers told Socrates how sad he was because he was being put to death with- out deserving it. But Socrates replied, smiling, that it would have been much worse if he had deserved it. He declared that no real harm could happen to a good man in this life or the next. The Greeks used to give poison to a condemned man, and allow him to drink it himself at any moment he might choose. Socrates drank the hemlock with his friends around him, and when they broke out in cries and tears he begged them to be quiet and allow him to die in peace.

It was not many years before the Athenians were very sorry indeed for the way Socrates had been treated, and those who had caused his death were punished. The death of Socrates came when Athens had fallen far from her greatness in the days of Pericles. In the days of Pericles he was still held in great honor.

It was in wars against the other states of Greece that Athens lost her riches and her power. Pericles knew that a struggle with Sparta must come, and he did all he could to strengthen Athens for the fight. He built the famous 'Long Walls' from Athens down to the sea, reaching the coast at the Piraeus, the port of Athens. No better plan could have been made for the safety of Athens. It would for the future be of little use for Sparta or any other state to besiege her by land, for food could always be brought in ships to the port, and then carried between the two Long Walls into the city. Twice in the early years of Pericles' rule Sparta had taken arms against Athens, but peace had been made.

It was not until two years before his death that the famous war between Sparta and Athens, known as the Peloponnesian War, broke out. The policy of Pericles had prepared Athens for the struggle, but she was weakened by jealousies among the members of the Confederacy of Delos, whom she had treated so proudly and so unjustly. Other causes helped to make Sparta win; and the later history of Athens, in its sad- ness and gloom, serves to throw into contrast her wonderful activity and prosperity in the age of Pericles.

The Greek Colonies in the West

Before continuing the history of the Greeks in Greece proper, it will be well to take a glance at what was happening to the Greek colonies farther west. It will be remembered that about the same time that Greeks had gone forth from Greece proper to make settlements on the coast of Asia Minor, others had sailed westward and made colonies in Sicily and the south of Italy. The Greeks loved to live in cities, and when possible near the sea, and so most of these towns were on the coast. Sicily and Southern Italy became known as Greater Greece, and the settlers never for- got that they were Greeks. They set up temples to the gods of their country, and lived much as they had done at home.

Some of these Greek colonies in Greater Greece were much richer than the Greek cities at home. So luxurious were the people of Sybaris, a town in South Italy, that even to-day we call a person who loves pleasure more than any- thing else a 'Sybarite.' A colony which went out from Sybaris itself was called

Croton, and became famous for its clever doctors. Pythagoras, a famous philosopher, belonged to Croton. The Sybarites and Crotonians always hated each other, and finally the Crotonians destroyed Sybaris completely in war; for these Greek states abroad were like those at home, always fighting with each other. Another colony famous for its luxury, although it was founded by men from Sparta, who must have been brought up in the strictest way, was Tarentum, on the gulf of the same name.

There were many Greek settlements in Sicily, the chief being Syracuse, founded by people from Corinth. Another great Greek settlement in Sicily was Agrigentum, which is remembered by its tyrant, Phalaris. He was a tyrant in our sense of the word as well as the Greek. He is said to have burnt his enemies alive inside a bull made of brass. After some years the people turned on him, and put him to death with terrible torture.

The Greeks in Sicily and Italy had changes of government very like the states in Greece proper. Some became aristocracies, some democracies, but they always remained city states, and were too jealous of one another ever to unite under one government. The people of Agrigentum built temples almost as beautiful as those of Athens, and their ruins are still to be seen. The most westerly of all the Greek settlements was Marsilia, in the south of France, now called Marseilles.

The Struggle with Carthage

It was a curious fact that at the same time that Greece proper was engaged in its life-and-death struggle with Persia, the Greeks of the west were also threatened by a great power. This was Carthage, a settlement made on the north of Africa long before by the Phoenicians in the days of their greatness. Phoenicia had long ceased to be a great power but Carthage had grown rich, and had herself sent out colonies. She had also won for herself much land along the north of Africa, partly consisting of other smaller Phoenician settlements, and partly to the native people, called the Libyans, with whom the Carthaginians mixed freely. The Libyans, however, had no part in the government, which was, in fact, in the hands of a few Carthaginian nobles. It was an aristocracy of the narrowest sort. The Carthaginians were rich and fond of pleasure, though the men who were actually ruling the state at any time lived plainly, and would not touch wine, thinking that a ruler should keep his brain clear and his wits sharp.

The Greeks and Carthaginians in the Western Mediterranean soon became very jealous of each other. There was a third state, higher up in Italy, Rome, which in the end was to conquer both, but her turn had not yet come. There were many small fights between the Carthaginians and Greeks, especially in Sicily, in the west of which the Carthaginians had made several settlements. The Greeks tried in the early part of the fifth century B.C. to push the Carthaginians out of Sicily altogether, but they did not manage it; and the Carthaginians in their turn chose the time when Xerxes was attacking Greece proper to make a determined attack on the Greeks in Sicily. They chose this time because they were afraid that otherwise the Greeks at home would come to the help of their colonies.

The Carthaginians made up their minds to send a great army, under Hamilcar, a brave soldier, who was a Carthaginian on his father's side and a Syracusan Greek on his mother's. Under his command were three thousand ships carrying an enormous army. It was an army much like that of Xerxes, awkward and unwieldy, too large because of the different peoples which went to make it up. There were Carthaginians and men from their colonies, the native Libyans, and some Greeks from states which were enemies of Himera, and the other Greek states of Sicily which were to be attacked. A storm destroyed many of the ships on their way across to Panormus (now Palermo), where Hamilcar landed his men and marched on Himera.

A great battle was fought, which the Greeks won, partly by a clever trick and partly by their better fighting. It was said that a hundred and fifty thousand men of the army of Carthage lay dead upon the field. Hamilcar watched the fight all day, burning a great fire of sacrifice to his gods, which may have been a sacrifice of human beings, for the Carthaginians had this dreadful practice. At sunset, seeing that defeat was certain, he threw himself into the fire and died, rather than return home to tell of his misfortune. All of the ships which had been drawn up upon the beach were burnt by the Greeks, and of the twenty which had not been drawn up, and so sailed away, only one returned to Carthage to tell the sad tale; for again a storm rose, and the others were destroyed.

The Greeks raised a monument in honor of Hamilcar, although he was their enemy, and the Carthaginians, although they were not usually grateful to their heroes, honored his memory for many years.

The soldiers who remained alive out of the army of Carthage were made slaves by the people of Agrigentum.

It was afterwards told that the battle of Himera was fought on the same day as the great sea-fight of Salamis. It was at any rate about the same time, and so the Greeks triumphed against their enemies in both east and west.

For seventy years after the battle of Himera the Carthaginians left the Greeks alone. If they had won Sicily, the Carthaginians might have won the south of Italy too. As it was, time was given for Rome to grow and extend its power there. The Greeks and Carthaginians were to have many a desperate struggle yet in Sicily ; but by that time the Greek power had become as nothing compared to that of Rome, and it was to Rome that the fall of Carthage was in the end due.

The Peloponnesian War

The history of this war, which lasted with periods of peace nearly thirty years, is perhaps of more importance in the history of Greece than in the history of the world. In it the power and greatness of Athens were brought to an end. It is just possible but not probable that if Athens had won she would have conquered the rest of Greece, and a great Athenian empire might have been formed. If this had been so, Athens would have had an even greater influence on later history than she has had. But it was not to be, and there is no real reason to believe that Athens, even if she had been victorious, would have set up such an empire. Still, the story of the war is interesting and important.

Ever since the Persian War, and especially under the rule of Pericles, Athens had irritated the other Greek states. She had made conquests on land, but these had been soon taken from her. But she clung to her empire, for such the Confederacy of Delos had become. The Persian power no longer threatened Greece, and had definitely set free even the Greek colonies in Asia Minor, but still Athens collected contributions from all the islands in the Aegean. The money was no longer kept at Delos, but was sent to Athens, and much of it was spent on the buildings there and on the amusement of the people.

Athens interfered also in the government of the other states of the confederacy whenever trouble arose, and set up democratic governments like their own. All important law cases had to be heard in Athens. When Samos, a large island which clung to its independence, refused to allow its quarrel with Miletus to be settled by Athens, the Athenians attacked her, destroyed all her walls of defense, took away her fleet, and made her pay the costs of the war. The Athenians kept sixty boats always in the Aegean Sea, as though she was afraid of a rebellion. For years a great struggle between Sparta and Athens had been expected. With Sparta necessarily went the whole of the Peloponnesian League, of which she was the chief member. The third greatest state in Greece was Corinth, which was a sea-power nearly as strong as Athens.

It was with Corinth that Athens first quarreled, but Sparta took the opportunity of calling a meeting to discuss a war with Athens. Messages were sent threatening war if the Athenians would not send Pericles away. This, of course, they would not do; but they might have sent peaceful messages back but for a speech which Pericles himself made to the people. He was a great speaker, and when he pointed out that the war was sure to come some day, and that the Athenians were quite strong enough to face their enemies, they made up their minds to fight, and to fight as Pericles should tell them.

So in the year 431 B.C. the great struggle between the two greatest states in Greece began. On the side of the Spartans were nearly all the Greeks of the peninsula, though Sparta's old enemy, Argos in the Peloponnesus, refused to join, and Plataea, the faithful little ally of Athens, fought once more on her side. The war began with an attack on Plataea by the people of Thebes. Three hundred Thebans got into Plataea, and kept the people shut up in their houses. But the Plataeans broke down the inside walls of their houses, and so were able to talk to each other. They arranged an attack on the Thebans, and a terrible fight took place. The Plataeans killed many Thebans, and many others were driven into a large building where, grain was kept. Other Thebans came up to the walls to help them ; but the Plataeans got them to go away, and then, in spite of their promises, killed every Theban left in the town. So angry were the people of Thebes that they sent another great army to attack Plataea, and the Athenians, although they were vexed that the Plataeans had broken their word, had to send an army to protect them from the Thebans.

Then the Spartans marched into Attica itself. Pericles thought that the Athenians would have little chance on land against the great army of Sparta, so he collected all the people of Attica within the Long Walls, for he knew that they could get plenty of food by sea.

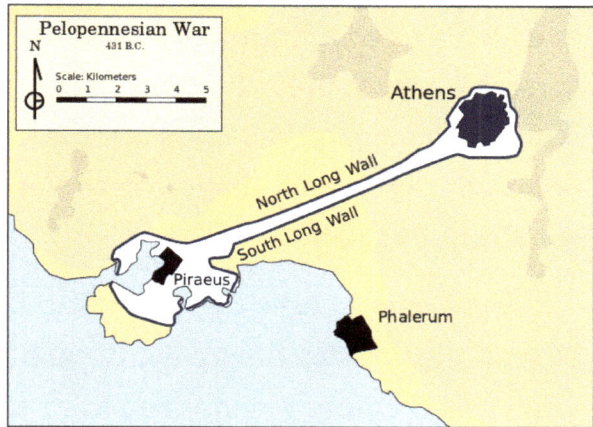

The people of Attica hated to leave their farms and vineyards to be destroyed by the enemy, but there was nothing else to do. The cattle were sent to the island of Euboea, and the people lived in huts and tents put up in haste in the empty space between the Long Walls. Then Pericles sent ships round to harass the people on the coasts of the Peloponnesus. The great Spartan army, once it had laid waste all the country round Athens, could do nothing more to harm the Athenians. Only a few bands of horsemen went out to hamper them. So the first year of the war ended. There was a great funeral service in memory of those who had been killed; and Pericles made a noble speech, assuring the Athenians that the severity of Sparta could never make men so noble as the freedom of Athens, and begging them not to grieve too much over the dead, but to be ready to die in their turn if need were.

The next year things happened in much the same way. In the spring (for ancient peoples never fought in the winter) a great Spartan army ravaged Attica again. The people of the countryside again took refuge between the Long Walls ; but a terrible misfortune fell upon the Athenians. A dreadful sickness called the plague broke out in the Piraeus. It came to Europe from the East, and had broken out in Egypt and also in Italy. It must have been brought by some ship to the Piraeus, and it spread quickly among the people crowded unhealthily together between the Long Walls. The people suffered terribly, and hundreds died, without any one to bury them. Pericles himself fell ill, but got better.

On all sides people began to grumble against him, as though their misfortunes were through his fault. A leather-seller called Cleon, a vulgar and ignorant man, tried to have the rule of Athens taken from him, but Pericles kept it till his death, which came shortly afterwards.

In the next year the Spartans took revenge on the little city of Platsea. All its men were killed, its women and children sold as slaves, and the city itself destroyed.

After the death of Pericles power in Athens fell to Cleon the leather-seller. He was very violent, and determined to remain at war, although many in Athens would have wished for peace. Just after his death, and after ten years of cruel and foolish warfare, a peace was at last made between Sparta and Athens. It lasted seven years, though it was made for fifty. Life in Athens had quite changed, and so had the spirit of the people. Socrates was still there, a relic of the great age of Pericles, but the new generation was changeable and fickle.

Alcibiades

Even when the fifty years' peace was signed, the best-known man in Athens was Alcibiades, a man thirty years old. His wayward character, his cleverness and courage, and his faults seem to be signs of the change which had come upon the Athenians. Alcibiades was a young relation of Pericles, and he was a pupil of Socrates, but he was not wise and serious like them. Knowing, as did Socrates, that the belief in the gods was not true, he merely laughed at them, whereas Socrates had taught men to look to higher things than these, and to do good even if they no longer honored the gods. Alcibiades was what is called irresponsible. He would do anything which came into his head at any moment. He often drank too much wine, and went noisily about the town with his companions. Yet it was to such a man as this that the Athenians now gave their trust. They mistook cleverness for wisdom.

At the first Olympic games after the fifty years' peace was signed, it was thought that Athens would not be able to send any people to take part. But Alcibiades was there offering sacrifices in beautiful golden bowls, and with seven four-horsed chariots to run in the races. Twice he was crowned as victor with the crown of wild olive. All the time Alcibiades was anxious that Athens should fight again with Sparta, and war did in fact soon break out again.

The Athenians at this time showed the greatest cruelty towards any member of the Confederacy of Delos which dared to rebel against her unjust empire. The Island of Melos, which rebelled, was conquered, and every man there was put to death, the women and children being sold into slavery.

Shortly after this the Athenians were induced by Alcibiades to send a great fleet and army to Sicily, where the colonies of Sparta were at war with other states. The Athenian expedition went to help a city called Egesta against another called Selinus. The people of Egesta had promised to pay the expenses of the expedition, and Alcibiades had persuaded the Athenians to agree. Nicias, another statesman in Athens, persuaded the people to send messengers to see if the people of Egesta were really as rich as they said. It was said after- wards that they showed the Athenian messengers plates and cups which were only gilded over, and pretended they were made of gold. The Athenians were deceived, and the expedition went off under Nicias and Alcibiades.

But the morning it sailed, the Athenians were shocked to find that all the busts of their god Hermes, which stood on little square pedestals at the street corners, had been thrown over and broken during the night. They came to the conclusion that this had been done by Alcibiades as a joke. It was nothing to him, because he did not believe in the gods, but to those who did it seemed a terrible sacrilege. Afterwards it was thought that perhaps Alcibiades had not done this thing after all, but he had done worse things against the gods. So messengers were sent after him to bring him back a prisoner in his own ship, but instead he sailed away to Sparta, and offered his services to the bitter enemy of his country.

The Sicilian expedition was a complete failure, for Alcibiades told to the Spartans all the plans of the Athenians, and persuaded them to send an army to fight against the Athenians in Sicily. He was full of anger against the men of his own state, and when he heard that sentence of death had been passed upon him, he declared, ' I will show them one day that I am still alive.'

The leadership of the Athenians in Sicily was left to Nicias, who had very little heart for it. Alcibiades had wished all the other Greek colonies in Sicily to join with the Athenians in an attack on the Spartan colonies, especially Syracuse, but most of them refused, and the Athenians were left practically alone. A great battle was fought in the immense harbor at Syracuse. The Athenians had many more ships than the Syracusans, but the Syracusans had placed theirs right across the mouth of the harbor, and the two hundred Athenian ships were hemmed in. All but sixty were destroyed, and the men who could escape joined the Athenian army on the shore. Nicias saw that they must give up the ships and try to escape by land to a part of the island where the people were friendly.

It was a terrible march, and the sick and wounded had to be left to die. Nicias, who had hated the whole thing, now showed how brave he was. Although he was very ill and tired, he went about among the men trying to cheer them. At one place the army had to march through a narrow pass between high rocks which the Syracusans fortified. For two days the Athenians fought, and then had to give up and choose another direction. They were short of food and water. At another place they caught sight of a river flowing in a deep hollow, and they were so thirsty that the whole army rushed forward to drink. Those in front were pushed down into the water, while those behind fell upon them, and were either crushed or pierced by the spears of the fallen. A Spartan army fell upon them while they were in this miserable state.

At last Nicias gave himself up with his army, begging that mercy should be shown to the ten thousand men who remained out of the forty thousand who had begun this terrible march. He promised that the Athenians would pay the Syracusans all that they had spent on the war. But the same cruelty was now shown as has been noticed in the later wars in Greece proper. The Athenians who thus gave themselves up were put in stone quarries, and left in hunger and cold. Nicias and the other Athenian leader, Demosthenes, were to be put to death, but preferred to kill themselves.

So ended in miserable defeat this expedition, planned in all light-heartedness by Alcibiades, and it was largely he who, by helping the Spartans, had ruined it. Meanwhile at home Sparta was still destroying and burning in the Plain of Attica. The Athenians were terribly distressed when they heard the sad fate of the Sicilian expedition. The loss of the ships was very bad for their navy, but they bravely set to work to build more. But the struggle was too severe. Nearly all the members of the Confederacy of Delos rebelled, and all the money of the League, so long stored up in Athens, was spent in fighting them. In

Athens itself the people had not even enough food. The
Persians once more began to fight against their old enemy
Athens, and joined with Sparta in helping the revolt of the
Athenian colonies in Asia Minor. Alcibiades had helped too in
this rebellion, but the Spartans were beginning to grow tired of
him. He had deceived one of their kings, and his liveliness of
character prevented them from really liking him. At last they
decided that he should die, but Alcibiades then joined the
friends of Athens, and fought against the colonies whom he had
encouraged to rebel. In the end he won several battles, and
then went back to Athens, was forgiven, and even welcomed.
His manner was as attractive to the Athenians as it was
unpleasant to the Spartans, and all his terrible treachery was
forgotten.

The Ruin of Athens

Alcibiades was a fine leader, but it was impossible to save
Athens. She was ruined on sea and on land. Alcibiades was
made head of the fleet, but he left it for a time under another
leader. During this time it was attacked and defeated by the
Spartan fleet, which was now bigger than that of Athens.
Alcibiades was ordered back to Athens to give an account of his
conduct, but he was afraid to go, and fled into Thrace. The
Spartans soon afterwards won another great victory at sea, and
took nearly the whole of the Athenian fleet prisoner.

Athens now gave up all hope, and after a terrible siege of
four months she was forced to give in to Sparta, who made
terribly hard conditions for peace. The Athenians had to destroy

the long walls and all their docks and their port at the Piraeus. They were to keep only twelve ships out of their once mighty fleet. They were not to attempt to gain power again over the members of the Confederacy of Delos, and indeed were not to have any possessions outside Attica. They must help Sparta for the future against all her enemies. The work of destruction of the long walls and the Piraeus was done by Spartan work- men, to the sound of music and rejoicing, and with every mark of insult to the Athenians.

So ended the Peloponnesian war, which had made Greece miserable for nearly thirty years. It was one of the most foolish and most useless wars in history. The Athens of Pericles was gone forever, and though the Athenians were still remarkable for their artists and scholars, there was never another chance of their taking the lead among the Greeks.

Alcibiades fled once more after the fall of Athens to the Persians, but the Spartans persuaded them to kill him. They set fire to his house, and when he ran out his enemies let fly a shower of arrows at him, and so killed him. His story is one of the strangest told of the great men of Greece. His cleverness and beauty do not make up for his selfishness and deceit. He was one of the chief causes of his city's downfall, though probably, if he had been allowed to lead the army in Sicily instead of being called back for punishment, he would have led it to victory. But he was hardly great enough to have conquered the Spartans, and even if he had done so he could never have made a great Greek empire with Athens at its head. Probably no one could have done this, though we cannot help wishing that it had been done, so that the learning and cleverness of the Athenians might have had an even greater influence on the world than they have had. As it was, Alcibiades, whom many of the Athenians had petted and admired, helped more than any other man to ruin the greatness of Athens.

The Last Days of Greek Independence

It might have seemed that now there was nothing to prevent Sparta uniting all the states of Greece in one empire. But this was not to be. The Spartans were hardly broad enough in the way they looked at things, and the Greek states were growing more and more jealous of each other. In a short time, when Thebes grew as powerful as Sparta, Athens was glad to join with Sparta against Thebes, a city which she had always hated because of its tyranny over her old friend Platsea. As time went on too, the Greeks nearly everywhere gave themselves up more and more to pleasure. Yet just at the end of the Peloponnesian war, some of them showed that they could still fight as well as in the days of Marathon and Thermopylae. The Spartans had during the war been friendly with various Persian princes, and now Cyrus, the brother of the Persian King Artaxerxes, asked permission of Sparta to collect an army in Greece, to help him in an expedition. He did not tell what the expedition was for, and many Greeks, who had been fighting at home and had nothing to do, joined him. In all there were thirteen thousand, and at their head was the Spartan Clearchus.

Xenophon's Great March

Among them was Xenophon, an Athenian and a pupil of Socrates. Cyrus led them with a great army of his own into the very center of the Persian empire, to Babylonia, to fight against Artaxerxes, kill him, and make himself king. The Greeks were surprised and angry when they found what he was doing, but they fought bravely, and chased the Persians opposed to them. But Cyrus himself was killed instead of his brother, and his army ran away. The Greeks were left alone, more than one thousand miles from home, with enemies all round them. The Persians were afraid of them, for they saw that a small army of Greeks was still more than equal to a large army of Persians. Artaxerxes sent one of his officers who pretended to be their friend, and offered to show them the way back to Greece. He got them safely out of Babylonia, and then asked their generals and captains to a meeting in his tent. Here men rushed upon them and killed them, and the army of ten thousand was left without their chief leaders in a strange land.

Most of them were nearly in despair, but Xenophon spoke to the chief men left, reminding them of the great victories which Greece had won over Persia, and begging them to fight their way home. And so they did. They had to march all that one thousand miles through strange countries where savage tribes attacked them, but they fought with them, and took food and went on, and at last they came within sight of the sea, and the brave men who had suffered so much, and so cheerfully, gave a great cry of joy, for they knew they were now within easy reach of home.

Afterwards, when he was safe in Greece, Xenophon wrote down the story of all the adventures he had passed through in the 'Retreat of the Ten Thousand.' A curious fact about Xenophon is that, though he was so brave and clever, he never had any love for Athens, his own city. He even once fought for the Spartans against the Athenians, when Athens was helping Thebes in a fight with Sparta.

The Spartans sent an army under one of their kings to fight the Persians in Asia Minor, and she also sent out a fine fleet, but Agesilaus, the king, was called back to fight Thebes, and Athens who had joined her. Athens had built her long walls again in spite of Sparta. Agesilaus defeated the army of Thebes and Athens, but meanwhile his fleet was destroyed by the Persians, with an Athenian to lead them, and Sparta gave up the idea of becoming a great sea-power. She also made peace with the Great King, who was left free once more to take as his own the Greek colonies in Asia Minor.

Sparta had set up in many cities of Greece a government like her own, and in Thebes among others. Two of the citizens who hated this government had been sent into exile, but they made up their minds to upset the government. They dressed themselves as hunters, and with their dogs came back to their city, and to their houses, without any one guessing who they were. Some of their friends gave a feast to the two governors, who ruled like the two kings in Sparta, and the exiles again dressed themselves up, this time as women, and went into the room where the rulers were eating. They were taken by surprise, and easily killed by the pretended women.

So the enemies of Sparta came into power. Athens sent help to Thebes, and the Thebans found a splendid leader in Epaminondas, one of the greatest heroes of Greek history. He was a splendid soldier, and a very noble character. He had not taken any part in killing the rulers set up by Sparta. He was clever too, and had studied philosophy, and in some ways was very like Pericles. As soon as the Thebans had become free themselves, they helped the other cities which Sparta had conquered to set themselves free. Epaminondas won a great victory over the Spartans, at Leuctra. In the battle Epaminondas used a quite new way of attacking the enemies' lines, and he is considered one of the world's great generals. Seven hundred Spartans were killed, and only three hundred Thebans, but Sparta pretended not to care, and forbade any public show of sorrow.

Epaminondas, the Hero of Thebes

The Thebans were now the chief people in Greece, but the other cities soon became as jealous of them as of Sparta, and the Spartans took advantage of this to make another attack on Thebes. Another great battle was fought at Mantinea. For a long time it seemed doubtful which of the splendid armies would win, but at last Epaminondas led a picked band of his best men in a determined dash on the enemy. The Spartan leader was wounded, and the Thebans won the battle, for soon afterwards the Spartans sent to ask permission to bury their dead, which meant that they owned that they were defeated.

But Epaminondas too was wounded to death. A javelin, a

sharp weapon with a pointed head of iron and a handle of wood, stuck in his breast. The wooden part broke off, and the doctors said that as soon as the head should be pulled out of his breast, the brave leader must die. But Epaminondas did not care at all so long as the victory was won. After his death peace was made, and for a short time no one Greek state tried to conquer the others. Even if he had lived, Epaminondas would never have been able to join all the Greeks together. He was like Alcibiades in that, a great soldier but not a very clever statesman. So Thebes, like Sparta and Athens, fell once more to the level of the other states. But there was a country to the north of Greece, which was not properly Greek, but which succeeded for a time where the Greeks had failed, and joined them together for a while, though against their will.

Greece and Macedonia

To the North of Greece proper lay a country which the Greeks called Macedonia. Its people were not pure Greeks, but some Greeks had probably mixed with them and married among them in early times. The Macedonian kings declared that they themselves belonged to an old Greek family belonging to the same group of Greeks as the Spartans. Certainly the kings and people of Macedonia had some of the best qualities of both Greeks and Barbarians. They were splendid fighters, and though the people were rough and uneducated, the kings had some idea of Greek learning and philosophy. Philip of Macedon, who was king at the time when Sparta and Thebes were fighting, had been, as a boy, for three years in Thebes. He had learned a great deal about Greece, and probably he then first got the idea of how easy it would be for a really strong power to conquer it. When he got back to his own country there was a great deal of quarrelling in the royal family as to who should be king, but Philip made himself king.

Macedonia had already a good army, but Philip made up his mind to make it even better. There were some fierce tribes in some parts of the country, and these he marched against and put in order. Macedonia was of course bigger than any of the Greek states, and Philip was able to get together an immense and splendid army.

Demosthenes,
a great Athenian Speaker

As soon as he felt strong enough, he began to take for himself some of the Greek colonies on the coast near Macedonia. Several of those belonged to Athens, but the Athenians did not try to prevent it. There was one states- man, however, in Athens, who grew passionately angry against Philip. This was Demosthenes, a very splendid speaker. He told the Athenians over and over again that this barbarian king of the North would soon try to conquer all Greece, if Athens and the other Greek states would not join to fight him in time. Philip gradually began to interfere in the new quarrels among the Greek states, and especially he helped to defend the temple of Apollo at Delphi, which had been attacked by the Phocians. He called himself a Greek and got some of the Greeks to say that Macedonia was a Greek state. He talked, too, very often of leading an army of all the Greek states (including Macedonia), with himself at its head, to fight the Persians as in the great days of Greece.

All the time Demosthenes was warning the Athenians against Philip. So bitterly did he hate him that he said he would rather have the Persians themselves. Even to-day, when any one speaks very angrily for a long time against anybody, we call such a speech a ' Philippic,' in memory of the long speeches in which Demosthenes tried to stir up the Athenians against Philip.

At last it became plain that the things which Demosthenes said against Philip were true and that he really meant to conquer all Greece. At last the Thebans and Athenians joined and fought a great battle with Philip at Chaeronoea. The Macedonian soldiers had always been brave, but before Philip had trained them they had had only shields made of wicker, and rusty swords. But Philip had taught them all that he had learned about fighting in Thebes, and the Greeks found that they had to fight against men who were stronger and better trained than themselves. Philip won a complete victory. He was very severe with the Thebans, but quite kind to the Athenians. He was now head of all Greece, but he did not live long to enjoy his power.

Philip was a strange mixture of Greek and Barbarian. He was of course brave and clever, and a great general. But he had some terrible faults. He was very fond of wine and often drank too much. When he was in this state he did and said very curious things. One day a woman came and asked him to settle a quarrel for her, and he settled it quite wrongly. The woman quietly said, 'I appeal.' 'To whom do you appeal?' asked the king. 'To Philip sober,' answered the woman. Philip saw that she was right, and now settled the quarrel quite differently. The saying 'To appeal from Philip drunk to Philip sober' is now a very common one.

Philip had several wives, imitating in this the Eastern kings. This was not a Greek custom, and in it Philip showed the Barbarian side of his character. His first wife was Olympias, who was also half a Greek. The people said she was a witch, and she was certainly very passionate and sometimes seemed almost mad. She and Philip quarreled terribly, and naturally she did not like his other wives. Philip and Olympias had a son called Alexander, who became king after his father, and is famous in history as Alexander the Great. Alexander took his mother's part in her quarrels, and was not very friendly with Philip.

It was during the rejoicings over the marriage of his daughter that Philip died, being killed by a young man who belonged to his bodyguard but thought that Philip had been unjust to him. During the marriage festival there was a procession to a theatre, where a play was to be held. Statues of the twelve great gods of Greece were carried in the procession, and behind them one of Philip himself, as though he too was a god. Then came the king, but just as he reached the door of the theatre the young man rushed forward and stuck a sword right through his body. Philip fell dead. The young man ran away, but tripped and fell and was killed by the king's friends. The Greeks rejoiced at Philip's death, but it did not free them from the Macedonians, for in Alexander they had to deal with a king as brave as his father and cleverer, and even more anxious for power. For the next few years the history of Greece must be told in connection with the wonderful story of Alexander the Great. (*Read more about Demosthenes on page 88.*)

Alexander the Great

Alexander, the son of Philip of Macedon, was only twenty years old when his father died. Demosthenes told the people of Athens that when he had seen him a few years before he was a dull boy. Demosthenes thought that the power of Macedon was at an end, but he can have been only a very poor judge of character. Alexander was a fine, handsome boy with a beautiful fair skin, blue eyes, and golden hair. There is a bust of him in the Museum of the Louvre at Paris, which shows him with fine shapely features and a noble forehead. Some people said that he was not the son of Philip at all, but that the god Jupiter was his father.

Alexander had of course a remarkable father and mother. In him can be seen his mother's power of imagination, with- out her tendency to madness. He had his father's ambition, courage, and power of ruling in a much higher degree. He soon showed the Greek cities that they could not throw off the Macedonian power. The city of Thebes, which dared to rise up against him, was destroyed, all but one house, that which had formerly belonged to the poet Pindar ; for Alexander, like his father, had great respect for the art and poetry of Greece. He was himself a pupil of Aristotle, the greatest of all the Athenian philosophers.

It is said that Alexander asked the Greeks in his army who were helping him against Thebes what should be done to that city, and it was by their advice that it was destroyed. Alexander himself was not generally cruel, but among these Greeks were men from Platsea, which had been by this time built up again, and they advised the destruction of Thebes in revenge for the destruction of their own city years before.

But the conquest of Greece was only one part of Alexander's work. He did not see why a Greek, as he called himself, should not conquer Persia as Persia had long ago tried to conquer Greece. He got together an army of thirty-five thousand men, and marched with them across the Hellespont. When he was half-way across, he killed a bull as a sacrifice to the god and goddesses of the sea, and poured wine from a golden cup into the water. When his ship drew near to the land, he flung a spear into the earth as a sign that he meant to win the land for his own.

The Persian leader who was sent to fight Alexander advised that his army should fall back before the Greeks and destroy everything on the way, so that Alexander and his army would have been without fojod. But his good advice was not followed, and the Persian army waited for the Greeks to come up to them. In order to reach them the Greeks had to cross the river Granicus, which was very deep in some places. Alexander's chief captain advised him to wait until the next morning before crossing, but

Alexander was too impatient. He said he would not be stopped by a little stream, and spurred his horse into the river. The whole army followed, and a great battle was fought on the other side. Alexander himself killed two of the Persian leaders and went into the very thickest of the fight. He would indeed have been killed but for the quickness of the captain of his bodyguard, named Clitus. One of the Persians was in the very act of bringing his sword down in a deadly blow on the head of Alexander, when Clitus swiftly cut off the hand which held the sword. Alexander won a great victory, and all Asia Minor submitted to him.

The men who had fought hardest on the Persian side were some Greek soldiers, who fought for money. When these were taken as prisoners, Alexander sent them home to work as slaves in Macedonia, for he said they were traitors to Greece. But he had the enemy's dead buried with all respect, like those of his own army who had been killed. He sent three hundred suits of armor, taken from the Persians, to be dedicated to the goddess Athene in the Acropolis of Athens, and had these words sent with them : 'From Alexander, son of Philip, and the Greeks (except the Lacedaemonians), out of the spoil of the foreigners inhabiting Asia.' The Lacedaemonians was another name for the Spartans. Alexander made an exception of them because they had refused to join in his expedition.

The Gordian Knot

At Gordium, one of the towns of Asia Minor which Alexander took, he was shown a chariot, said to belong to the man who had founded the city. It was tied up with cords which were fastened in a knot which, it was said, no one could undo. Alexander took his sword and solved the difficulty by cutting the cord across. It was said that the man who undid the knot should conquer the world.

A second great battle was fought next year at the river Issus. This time the Persian king was there. He was another Darius by name. The Persian army is said to have had six hundred thousand men in it, but it was one of the immense useless armies of unwilling soldiers which the Greeks had met and conquered so often. The dashing attack of Alexander scattered it, and Darius himself ran away.

Alexander seized the Persian camp, and among others the mother, wife and daughter of Darius were taken prisoners. They were crying because they thought the king had been killed, but Alexander told them that he had got safely away, and so comforted them. Alexander was nearly always kind and polite to his enemies when they were in his power.

He next took all the coast of Syria and Phoenicia, but the old city of Tyre, though it would have submitted to him, refused to let him enter the city to sacrifice to one of its gods. Alexander was terribly angry and besieged the city for seven months. He brought Phoenician ships to help him, and when at last Tyre had to give way, Alexander allowed his soldiers to kill most of the men in cold blood on the seashore. The women and children were sent into slavery. Alexander was terribly angry when his pride was offended, as it had been in this case. He sacrificed at the shrine, but there was little to be proud of in this victory.

Darius was not a very strong or brave king. He was now thoroughly frightened, and sent word to Alexander that he would give up to him all the land west of the river Euphrates if he would only let him live in peace beyond that river. But even such an immense empire could not satisfy Alexander. His chief captain Parmenio said to him, 'If I were Alexander I should agree to this rather than rush into further dangers.' 'And so should I,' replied Alexander, 'if I were Parmenio.'

But he was not. He was full of imagination, and seems to have thought it possible to join the East and West in one great empire. It was not possible, for, as can be seen through all history, the people of the East are quite different from those of the West. They have a quite different way of thinking about things. But Alexander did come nearer than anybody to joining the two.

At the town of Gaza Alexander again met with resistance, and he treated it with the same cruelty as Tyre. It is said that he went to Jerusalem and prayed in the temple. The Jews welcomed him, for they had suffered much under Persian rule, and they showed him the place in the Book of Daniel which says that a Greek would conquer the Persians. After- wards when Alexander built the city of Alexandria, called after himself, he invited many Jews to settle there.

From Asia Minor Alexander marched into Egypt, which gave in to him immediately. It was on an island at the mouth of the Nile that he built Alexandria, which in time became the second greatest city in the world at the time when Rome was the greatest. From Egypt in the spring Alexander led his men right across Asia beyond the Euphrates through Mesopotamia, and across the Tigris, and there at last met the army of Darius. The battle was fought not very far from the town of Arbela, and is known as the battle of Arbela. Darius had had his army standing all night, for it was so large that he was afraid that if the soldiers lay down to sleep he would never get them into order again. The Macedonians had a good night's sleep and were quite fresh for the fight. The army of Darius was rather different from the usual Persian armies. It had in it 50,000 paid Greek soldiers and men from wild tribes of the very East. There were elephants too which the Greek soldiers had never seen. Then again the land beyond the Euphrates had always been considered dangerous by the Greeks, and here they were beyond the Tigris as well. But Alexander's soldiers had the greatest trust in him and no one grumbled. The fight was fast and furious, but at last the Persian army fell into confusion, and Darius once more fled from the field. Alexander marched on to Babylon and then to the great Persian capital, Susa, and took it for his own. At Susa Alexander, having, it is said, drunk too much wine, burnt down the royal palaces. In them were wonderful books full of the writings of the great Persian philosopher Zoroaster and of the history of the Persian empire. These were lost for ever to the world, and many things written in these books can never now be known. Alexander was bitterly sorry afterwards, and indeed it

was one of the worst acts of his life, and we find it hard to forgive him for it. He then marched after Darius, who was running away with Bersus, one of his relations. For weeks Alexander followed him, and when at last Darius, who was worn out and weary of the struggle, knew that he would be caught, he told Bersus and his friends that he would give himself up to Alexander. But Bersus was an ambitious man, and as he knew that with Darius as a prisoner Alexander would be surer than ever of keeping Persia for his own, he turned and stuck his sword in Darius and killed him, and then fled on. Darius was found dying by one of Alexander's soldiers, and he begged him to thank Alexander for being so kind to his wife and daughter. Alexander buried Darius with all honor in the old tomb of the Persian kings.

Alexander in India

In four years Alexander had won for himself the great empire of Persia. But he was not yet satisfied. He stayed only to make things orderly and safe, and then marched through mountain passes into the great unknown continent of India. He conquered the land now known as the Punjab, and had a famous struggle with a prince called Porus. Porus was almost a giant. He had an enormous elephant on which he used to ride into battle. When its master could no longer fight, the elephant would lie gently down, let him slide from its back, and pull the arrows from its body with its trunk. Porus was defeated and taken prisoner. Alexander asked him how he wished to be treated. He quietly answered, 'Like a king.' Alexander was so pleased with the answer that he gave Porus his kingdom back, and even some more land to make it larger. But of course Porus had to own that Alexander was over him. Alexander, too, had a faithful animal which he loved very much. This was his horse Bucephalus, which he had ridden for many years. Alexander always tried to save it from too much work or any pain, but he always rode it in battle. It was wounded in the battle, and died soon afterwards. Alexander built a city on the spot where it was buried, and called it Bucephalia after the horse.

Alexander would probably have wished to add all India to his empire, but at last his army began to rebel, and would not follow him any farther. He led them back through the passes of North-West India, and across Asia once more to Susa, and from there to Babylon. Here he fell suddenly ill of a fever and died. He was only forty-two years old. In the ten years that he had been in Asia, he had won contests such as no man has done before or since. We can only imagine what he would have done had he lived longer.

He was one of the greatest men who ever lived. Besides being a wonderful soldier and leader of men, he was generally kind and he admired noble things. Of course he was sometimes cruel, and when really angry he was quite as savage and uncivilized as any of his enemies. It is dreadful to think that he killed in anger his great friend Clitus, who had saved his life at the battle of Granicus. In anger he was more Barbarian than Greek. But he lived in a savage time, and we must remember that the Greeks, who had been civilized for hundreds of years, were almost equally cruel. With all his faults, the name of Alexander the Great and the story of his life will always remain to fill men with wonder.

The End of Alexander's Empire

As soon as Alexander was dead his great empire broke up, and his generals made themselves kings of different parts of it. Some of these rulers very soon lost much of their Greek character, and became very much like the people they ruled. In time most of them were conquered by the Roman people, who soon after this became a great conquering nation. The cities which Alexander had built, and the colonies of Greek soldiers which he had left everywhere, taught the Eastern people something of Greek civilization. Alexandria became almost a second Athens, famous for its learning and its philosophy. Macedonia became a kingdom, and after many quarrels the family of one of his generals, Antigonus, got the kingship, and it remained in the family for more than a hundred years, when Macedonia was conquered by Rome and made part of the Roman empire.

After the death of Alexander the Greeks tried to free themselves from the power of Macedonia, but the Macedonian ruler marched against them and made them give in. Demosthenes, who had spent so many years in the struggle against the kingdom which he hated so much, and had hoped that now at last the Greeks would be free, now poisoned himself in despair.

After about fifty years some of the smaller states of Greece, which had never before taken much part in her history, joined together into leagues, and for the first time there was

something like equality between the states of Greece. These smaller states were content to be equal with each other, and did not try to conquer other states like Sparta and Athens and the great states of earlier times. But they could never make Greece really great again, and even now there were jealousies. At last Sparta, who had always been ready to join with the enemies of Greece when she was angry and jealous, called in the Romans against the Achaean League, with which she was quarrelling. The Romans came and settled the quarrel by making Greece a province of her empire. This was in the year 146 B.C. The history of the next few hundred years is the history of this wonderful Roman people which had grown up from a city-state in the middle of Italy into a great nation, and then into an empire the greatest the world has ever known. We must turn back more than six hundred years to tell the tale of the Roman people from the beginning.

Lycurgus

I

About eighty years after the Trojan War the descendants of Hercules with a large band of followers invaded the Peloponnesus, or southern part of Greece, where Agamemnon and Menelaus had once lived. They captured Sparta and made it their capital and after that called themselves Spartans.

The Spartans made slaves of people who were already living in the country and called them Helots or captives. The conquerors divided the land among themselves and made the Helots work their farms.

After about three hundred years had passed it seems that some of the Spartans had grown rich, while others had lost their land and slaves and become poor.

The Spartans who had lost their property were not willing to work like the slaves, and sometimes, when they had no bread for their children, bands of them marched through the streets of Sparta, broke into the houses of the rich and took whatever they could lay their hands on.

During one of these riots, one of the two kings,—for the Spartans always had two kings with equal power,—went out of his palace to stop it. He tried to persuade the people to go quietly home, but they paid no attention to him and a butcher in the crowd rushed up and stabbed him.

The murdered king left two sons. The elder became king, but

soon died. The younger was one of the wisest and best men that ever lived in Greece. His name was Lycurgus and after his brother's death every one wished him to become king. But an infant child of the late king was the rightful heir, and Lycurgus refused to be anything more than regent.

For a while he ruled in the young king's name, but some people accused him of wishing to make himself king. So he gave up the regency and went traveling. He visited many lands and studied their plans of government. After being absent several years he came back to Sparta. There he found that the rich were richer and the poor were poorer and more unhappy than when he went away. Everyone turned to him as the only man from whom help could come.

He persuaded the people to let him make new laws for Sparta. The first change that he made was to give every Spartan a vote. There was a Senate of Thirty which might propose laws, but all the citizens were called together to pass or reject them.

Next he persuaded the rich people to divide their land fairly among all the citizens. So now no one had more than he needed, but every one had a farm large enough to raise wheat or barley, olive oil and wine for his family for a year. No Spartan was permitted to work or to engage in any trade, but the slaves were divided, so that every Spartan had slaves to work for him.

Besides the Spartans and the slaves there was another class of men living on the lands of Sparta who were not slaves like the Helots, and yet not citizens like the Spartans. These men were farmers, traders and mechanics. They had to pay taxes and fight when called upon, but neither they nor the Helots had anything to say about the government. There were about 10,000 pure Spartans and about 140,000 in the two lower classes, so you will see that the political power in Sparta was in the hands of a very few men. Their government was what we call an "oligarchy," which means a government by the few.

II

LYCURGUS did not wish the Spartans to become traders and grow rich, and it is said that he ordered their money to be made of iron. This iron money was worthless outside of Sparta, so the traders of other countries would not take it in payment for their goods and sold nothing to Spartans.

In those days soldiers fought chiefly with swords and spears; therefore no matter how brave men were, they had to have physical strength to win a victory. Lycurgus made laws that the men and boys of Sparta should be trained in running, boxing, wrestling, throwing quoits, hurling javelins, and shooting with bows and arrows. The girls had nearly the same training.

The feeble and deformed were thought by Lycurgus to be useless. Infants were therefore examined and those that were weak or deformed were not allowed to live. A strong, well-formed infant was handed back to its

parents with the order, "Bring up this child for Sparta."

Boys remained at home until they were seven years old. Then they were taken in charge by the State to be trained. The clothing given them was scanty. They went about with their heads and feet bare, and slept on hard beds, or even on floors, with rushes instead of a mattress.

To teach the boys temperance Helots were sometimes purposely made drunk. Thus the boys saw how foolish men become when they drink too much.

One lesson that every Spartan boy had to learn was to endure pain without flinching. Another was that in battle a man might die, but must not surrender. When the young Spartan was leaving home for the field of battle his mother would hand him his shield and say, "Come back with this, or upon this."

Lycurgus was opposed to all expensive ways of living. He thought that luxury was a waste of money and made men weak and effeminate. He made a law that the men should not take their meals at home but in a public dining hall; and there only the simplest kind of food was set before them—bread, cheese, olive oil, and a kind of black broth that was probably made of black beans. Figs and grapes served for dessert. It is said that some rich people were very angry because they had to eat at the public tables and that one young man stoned Lycurgus.

A great change came over the Spartans after they had adopted the new laws and ways of living. Instead of being a nation of idlers they became so strong and brave that when there was talk of building a wall round the city, Lycurgus said, "Sparta's citizens are her walls."

When Lycurgus saw what improvement had been made he told the people that he was going on a long journey. He made them promise that they would not change his laws until he returned.

He never returned. When the Spartans felt sure that he was dead they built a temple in his honor and worshiped him as a god. He left Sparta about 825 B.C. and his laws were not changed for several hundred years. They made Sparta the greatest military state in Greece.

Militiades the Hero of Marathon

I

AFTER Pisistratus died his two sons, Hippias and Hipparchus, ruled over Athens. They governed well until Hipparchus was killed by his enemies. Then Hippias became so cruel that the Athenians banded together and drove him out of the city.

Some time after being driven from Athens Hippias sailed to Asia and begged Darius, king of Persia, to help him regain his power. At that time Persia was the greatest country in the world. Darius, her sovereign, was called "the Great King," or simply "the King," as if there were no other king on the face of the earth. He intended that there should be no other if he could have his way. He made up his mind not only to help Hippias, but also to make himself master of Greece. Persian heralds were therefore sent to every state of Greece to demand from each a tribute of earth and water. If the Greeks had yielded to this demand it would have been the same as saying that all the land and water of Greece belonged to Persia. Some of the states submitted, others proudly refused. The Athenians threw the heralds into a ditch into which the bodies of criminals were thrown; the Spartans threw them into a well and told them, "There you will find both earth and water for your master."

As soon as Darius heard of this he declared war and a little later his fleet, carrying one hundred and fifty thousand men, set sail for Greece. The Persians landed on the Grecian coast and went into camp on the plain of Marathon, twenty-two miles from Athens.

Meantime the Athenians had not been idle. They had collected a force of ten thousand men, and the entire army was under ten generals, each of whom in turn was commander-in-chief for one day. The little city of Platæa, unasked, had sent a thousand volunteers.

The ablest of the Greek generals was Miltiades. He determined to attack the enemy at once, and when his day of command came, on the 12th of August, 490 B.C., he drew up the Greek army in line of battle and moved across the plain. Then he charged upon the Persian army, broke their line, and drove them back to their ships in confusion.

News of the victory was carried to Athens by a soldier, who though wounded ran the twenty-two miles from the field of battle to the city. Reaching the market-place, he rushed into the crowd of citizens assembled there, and crying—"Rejoice! Rejoice! We are victors!"—fell dead.

This news delighted all loyal Athenians, but was very unwelcome to some traitors who had been hoping to hear of a Persian victory. These traitors had gone to a mountain near Athens, and with a polished shield they flashed to the Persian fleet a signal to sail to Athens and capture the city before Miltiades could return from Marathon.

Fortunately, the signal was seen in the camp of the Greeks. Miltiades guessed what it meant and marched back to Athens immediately. So when the Persians approached in their ships they found that if they landed they must again meet the army of Miltiades. They had no wish to do this and sailed away across the Ægean Sea to the Great King's own dominions.

The battle of Marathon showed that the Greeks were equal to any soldiers in the world. They had routed an army of Persians fifteen times as large as their own, and had lost only one hundred and ninety-two men.

The Greeks believed that this splendid victory was won through the aid of their gods and of their god-like hero Theseus, who was said to have fought in the thick of the battle and made terrible havoc among the Persians.

II

MILTIADES won great fame in Athens. Honors were showered upon him and whatever he asked was granted. Thinking that he could add still more to his own glory and that of Athens, he asked that a fleet of seventy ships be placed at his command and that he be allowed to do with it as he pleased.

The fleet was granted and with it he set sail for the island of Paros. The people of Paros had helped the Persians in the recent war and Miltiades wished to punish them, but he also hoped to avenge himself upon a personal enemy. The expedition was a complete failure. The town of Paros was not captured, and Miltiades was obliged to give up the siege and return to Athens.

Moreover at Paros his thigh had been badly hurt while he was leaping over a fence so that he came home injured as well as unsuccessful. Upon his return he was accused of having deceived the people and wasted the public money.

When his trial took place he was brought before his judges upon a couch, being too weak to stand or sit. The decision of the court was against him and he was sentenced to pay a heavy fine, which he was too poor to pay. Not long afterward he died of the injury that he had received at Paros.

After the death of Miltiades the Athenians were sorry for their harshness toward him. Remembering only his heroism at Marathon, they buried him with the highest honors on the plain where his great victory was won.

Themistocles

I

AT this time the leading man of Athens was a great

statesman and soldier named Themistocles. Some years before when the news had come that Xerxes was collecting an army and intended to invade Greece, the Athenians sent messengers to Delphi to ask the oracle what they should do. Delphi was upon the side of Mount Parnassus, and there stood a temple of Apollo. It was built over the cleft in the rock which, you remember, Deucalion found long ago as he and Pyrrha were coming down the mountain after the flood.

In the inner chamber of the temple just over the cleft, was a three-legged stool called a tripod. When a person wished to consult the oracle the priestess, who was called the Pythia, took her seat on the tripod. In a few minutes her eyes would close and she would begin to talk. The words which she spoke were noted, and the Greeks believed that they were really the words of the god Apollo.

Her answer to the messengers from Athens was:

"When everything else in the land of Cecrops shall be taken Jupiter grants to Minerva that the wooden wall alone shall remain undestroyed, and it shall defend you and your children. Stand not to await the attack of horses and foot from Asia, but retire. You shall live to fight another day. And thou, O divine Salamis, shalt destroy the children of women!"

What do you think this strange answer meant? The Athenians were greatly puzzled by it.

Themistocles said that the "wooden wall" meant ships of war, and that the gods would save the people if they would leave their city and trust to their fleet when the enemy approached.

He advised the Athenians to build more ships of war. The people at last came to believe him. Rich Athenians gave him money, and the people voted that the silver which was dug every year from the silver mines owned by the city should be used to pay for building ships of war. And thus by the time Xerxes began his march Athens had a fleet of two hundred ships of war. These vessels were gigantic rowboats, each having as many as a hundred and fifty oars. Each had also a mast with a single big sail, which was hoisted to help the rowers.

The capture of Thermopylae had given the Persians an open road to Athens, and so the women and children of the city and the men who were too old to fight had been sent away in merchant ships to places of safety. A few men stayed in Athens and defended the citadel, as you learned in the last chapter. The rest went out in the war ships with Themistocles to fight behind the "wooden wall."

II

THEMISTOCLES and the commanders of the fleets of the other Greek states took their vessels into the narrow strait of Salamis, which lay between the island of Salamis and the shore of Attica. Here the Persians followed them. Themistocles now wished the Greeks to give battle to the Persians, but the Spartan commander and the other Greek leaders were unwilling to risk a battle in the narrow strait. They proposed to retreat. Themistocles was determined, however, that a battle should be fought in the strait; so he sent word secretly to Xerxes that the Greek ships were going to try to get away and advised him to head them off. Xerxes was delighted to get this message, and during the night he sent a part of his fleet up the shore of Attica to the other end of the strait, so as to hem the Greek fleet in between two lines of Persian ships. Next morning the Greek leaders all saw that there was nothing to do but fight, and at once their ships were drawn up in line of battle.

Xerxes' throne had been placed on a high cliff on the shore of Attica, so that he might look down upon the battle. When the sun rose he took his seat upon the throne. He was clothed in his royal robes and surrounded by the princes of his court. Below him were a thousand Persian war vessels, while close to the shore of the island lay three hundred and seventy-eight Greek vessels. It seemed an easy victory for the Persians. The Greeks rowed forward from the shore of Salamis, shouting the cry, "We fight for all." The Persians replied with their war cry, and the battle began. For a time the Persians had the advantage. But their ships were in the way of one another; those in the front could not go back, those in the rear could not come forward. The confusion became terrible. Ship after ship of the Persians sank, some of them rammed by the Greeks, others run down by their own allies. In all two hundred Persian vessels were destroyed and a great number captured, while the Greeks lost only forty.

When Xerxes saw his thousand vessels sunk or captured or rowing away in flight, he determined to go back to Persia.

He at once returned to northern Greece, where he left 300,000 men in command of his brother-in-law, Mardonius. With the rest of his army he marched on to the Hellespont.

Here he found that storms had destroyed his bridges, so that what was left of his army was carried across to the shore of Asia Minor in ships.

III

EVERYBODY in Greece now admitted that Themistocles had been right in his explanation of the oracle that the "wooden wall" would save the people. And "Salamis," as the oracle had said, "destroyed the sons of women"; but they were chiefly the sons of Persian, not Grecian women.

The battle of Salamis brought fresh glory to Themistocles. After some years, however, he became unpopular and was banished from Athens. He stayed at Argos. Then the Spartans, who were his enemies, accused him of treason against Greece. Fearing that he could not get a fair trial at Athens he fled to Persia.

The Persian king gave him three cities to support him, and in one of these he lived until his death in 453 B.C.

Aristides the Just

I

ARISTIDES was the rival of Themistocles. Themistocles was

wise and brave, but selfish and fond of money. Aristides, too, was wise and brave, but he was also so honorable that the Athenians called him "the Just."

On one occasion he was acting as judge between two men. One of them had spoken unfairly of Aristides and the other came secretly to Aristides to tell him of it. "My friend," said Aristides, "tell me the wrong the man has done to you, not what he has done to me. It is not my cause that I am to decide, but yours."

Aristides opposed many plans that Themistocles wished to carry out, and so at length Themistocles determined to have him banished.

There was at Athens a curious way of getting rid of a citizen. Every year this question was put before the people: "Does the safety of the State require that any citizen shall be banished?" If it was decided that this was necessary the people were called upon to vote. No person's name was mentioned, but every citizen wrote on a small earthenware tablet the name of any man whom he thought dangerous to the state. The tablets were collected and counted, and if the name of any one man was written on as many as 6,000 tablets he had to leave the city for ten years. Banishing people in this way was called "ostracism." We often use the word to-day. It comes from a Greek word meaning an earthenware tablet.

Themistocles and his friends persuaded many of the Athenians that Aristides was a dangerous citizen. So when a public meeting was being held the people were asked if they thought any citizen ought to be banished. No one mentioned Aristides' name, but Themistocles' friends said, "Let a vote be taken." While the vote was being cast a countryman who could not write his own name came up to Aristides and said:

"Friend, will you write the name of Aristides for me on this tablet?"

"Has Aristides ever wronged you?" asked Aristides gently.

"No," said the other, "I have never even seen him, but I am tired of hearing him called 'the Just.' "

Aristides said no more, but wrote his own name on the tablet.

There were enough votes against Aristides to banish him. As he was leaving Athens he prayed the gods that the time might never come when his fellow-citizens should have cause to be sorry for what they had done.

That time came, however. Three years later when Athens was threatened by the Persians the citizens, at the request of Themistocles himself, recalled Aristides. He sailed from his place of exile to the bay of Salamis and went on board the ship of Themistocles only a few hours before the famous battle. Themistocles at once gave him command of one of the Athenian ships, and he did good service in the battle.

II

IN the spring following the battle of Salamis Mardonius, the Persian commander who was in Thessaly, tried to bribe the Athenians to become allies of the great king but they refused his offers with scorn. He then marched to Athens and the people abandoned the city, so that it fell into his hands.

The Greeks, however collected an army of one hundred and ten thousand men. Pausanias, a nephew of Leonidas, the hero of Thermopylae, was made commander-in-chief; but Aristides commanded the Athenian troops. Mardonius now retreated from Athens, destroying and burning as he went. The Greeks followed and overtook him near the city of Platæa, and there they defeated him in one of the "decisive battles of the world." Mardonius himself was killed.

It took ten days to divide the spoil and bury the dead. A tenth of the spoil was sent to Delphi and dedicated to Apollo, because the promise of his oracle that "the wooden wall would save the city" had led to the great victory of Salamis. A temple was erected to Minerva, and thank-offerings were made to other gods. "Liberty games" were established, to be held on the battlefield once in four years, and every year the tombs of those who had fallen in battle were to be decorated with flowers. The land upon which Platæa stood was declared to be sacred and the inhabitants of the city were to be always free from attack by other Greeks.

On the afternoon of the very day on which the battle of Platæa was won the Greek fleet gained a great victory over the Persians at Mycale, on the coast of Asia Minor. After their defeats at Marathon, at Platæa, and at Mycale, the Persians never again attempted to conquer Greece.

III

AS soon as the victory at Platæa had freed Greece from the

ravaging Persian army, the Athenians flocked back to their ruined city and began to rebuild it. Aristides and Themistocles carried on this work hand-in-hand.

It was found that the sacred olive tree on the Acropolis, though burned to the ground, was not killed. From its root had sprung a stout young shoot. This was taken by the citizens as a good omen and rebuilding of the city went on rapidly. The great sea-port called the Piræus was fortified, and a wall was built round the city.

These and other public works required a great outlay of money, and it was needful to put some one whom all the citizens trusted in charge of the fund raised. Aristides was chosen and enormous sums of money were placed in his hands. He used his office solely for the good of the people and never became rich.

When he died, about 468 B.C., the whole nation mourned and he was buried at public expense.

Pericles

I

CIMON had a rival named Pericles who was the most able leader Athens ever had. He had the power of a tyrant but he used it for the welfare of the people.

He had many excellent laws passed. One was that a man accused of any crime should be tried by a certain number of his fellow-citizens. This was like our trial by jury, and it gave an Athenian the same rights in a trial that an American citizen has today. Another good law proposed by Pericles was that any citizen who fought in the army or navy of Athens should be paid for doing so. Still another of his laws was that if a poor man wished to go to the theater he might get the money from the city treasurer to pay for his seat.

You will remember that Themistocles and Aristides began to rebuild and beautify Athens after it had been burned by the Persians. This work was afterward carried on by Pericles. It was said that he found the city of brick and left it of marble.

Under his orders the white marble Parthenon, or temple of Minerva, was erected on the Acropolis. It was one of the most beautiful buildings in the world.

In front of it stood a bronze statue of Minerva, so large that it could be seen far out at sea. Within was a splendid statue of the goddess, nearly thirty feet high, which was of ivory and gold.

Pericles made Athens strong as well as beautiful. He finished the "Long Walls" which Cimon had begun. These walls were built from the city to her ports, which were about four miles away. Between two of the walls was a roadway, by which in time of war provisions could be safely carried from the harbor to the city.

Sparta was not pleased to hear of the fortifications of her rival. Athens might make herself beautiful if she chose, but she must not make herself strong. The Spartans watched for an opportunity to quarrel with the Athenians, and the opportunity soon came. The people of Corcyra, an island now called Corfu, lying off the west coast of Greece, went to war with the people of Corinth. Athens helped the Corcyreans; Sparta, the Corinthians.

This was the beginning of a contest between Sparta and Athens which desolated Greece for twenty-seven years (431 B.C. to 404 B.C.) It is called the Peloponnesian War, because most of the states in the Peloponnesus took part in it and were allies of Sparta. Athens also had her allies.

Athens was well prepared for war. She had a large sum of money in her treasury, a good fleet, and about thirty thousand soldiers whom she could put into the field.

The Spartans brought a force of sixty thousand men into Attica to attack Athens. Pericles then urged the country people to leave their farms and homes and come into the city. They took his advice, and every vacant spot in Athens was filled with huts and tents. Pericles thought that Athens, protected by the "Long Walls," could stand any siege.

In this he was right, for the Spartans made no headway; but very soon the Athenians were attacked by a foe far more terrible than the Spartans. This was "the plague." So many people were huddled together in the city that it was impossible to keep it clean and healthy. People began to sicken and die by dozens, then by hundreds. The Spartans, fearing that the plague might attack them, retreated across the Isthmus of Corinth into Peloponnesus.

While Athens was in this desperate condition Pericles acted most nobly. The plague carried off his eldest son, his sister, and many of his closest friends. Yet he went among the people, calming and cheering them, and attending faithfully to the affairs of the government. It was only when he laid the funeral wreath upon the lifeless body of his favorite son that he broke down and sobbed and shed a flood of tears.

While the Spartan army was threatening Athens, and when the plague came, many of the Athenians blamed Pericles. But when he was in sorrow all Athens showed him the greatest respect and affection.

Not long after the death of his son, he himself was stricken with a fatal illness. As he lay dying one of those at his bedside spoke of the good that he had done for Athens.

"What you praise in my life," he said, "has been due to fortune. I deserve no credit for it. That of which I am proudest is that no Athenian ever wore mourning because of anything done by me."

His death occurred in the third year of the Peloponnesian War. It was a sad blow to the Athenians, for he was the greatest of all their statesmen.

II

One of the friends of Pericles was Phidias, the sculptor who molded the bronze figure of Minerva that stood in front of the Parthenon. He carved also the ivory and gold statue of the goddess that was inside the building.

His fame spread over all Greece, and he was invited to adorn the temple of Jupiter at Olympia. For this temple he made his masterpiece. It represented Jupiter seated upon his throne. The statue was so perfect that it was considered one of the wonders of the world.

When Phidias, after several years absence, returned to Athens he was persecuted by the enemies of Pericles, because he was known to be a friend of the great statesman. He was first accused of having stolen part of the gold which had been supplied by the city to decorate the statue of Minerva. Fortunately, when Phidias was working upon the statue Pericles had advised him to fasten the gold on in such a way that at any time it could be taken off and weighed. It was now removed and weighed and the weight was found to be exactly what it should be.

Phidias was then charged with having insulted the goddess Minerva, because he had carved upon her shield a likeness of himself and one of Pericles. On this charge he was cast into prison to await trial.

Before the day of trial came, however, the great sculptor was taken sick and died.

III

Under Pericles Athens was at the height of her glory, and the twenty-eight years during which he was at the head of Athenian affairs are known in history as "The Golden Age of Pericles." At no other time were there in Athens so many great painters, sculptors, writers, and philosophers.

A celebrated historian who lived during the age of Pericles was Herodotus. He is called "the Father of History."

Another famous historian of those days was Thucydides, who wrote a history of the Peloponnesian War.

Lysander

THE admiral of the Spartan fleet in the last years of the Peloponnesian War was a man named Lysander. He was brave, but he was also cunning and frequently gained the victory by laying a trap for his enemy. It is said that he used to tell his officers, "When the lion's skin is too short you must patch it with that of a fox." This was another way of telling them that if they could not succeed by force they must try cunning.

After Alcibiades had been dismissed from the command of the Athenian fleet a commander named Konon was appointed to succeed him. Lysander decided to set a trap for him. The two fleets came in sight of each other off the shore of the Hellespont, near a place called Ægos Potamos, which means Goat's River. One morning, at break of day, Lysander drew up his ships in line as though he intended to give battle. Later in the day the Athenians rowed toward the Spartans and challenged them to fight, but not a Spartan vessel moved. The Athenians concluded from this that the Spartans were either not prepared to fight, or were afraid.

The next day the challenge was again given by the Athenians, and again the Spartans paid no attention to it. The same thing happened the third day and the fourth. By this time the Athenians felt sure that Lysander was afraid of them. Many therefore went on the shore, some in search of provisions, some to take a stroll, some to sleep. Only a small guard was left with the fleet.

As soon as Lysander saw that the Athenians ships were unprotected he rowed swiftly to the place where they were lying and captured nearly the whole fleet. Of one hundred and eighty ships only about ten escaped. Three or four thousand men were taken prisoners, and all were put to death.

One of the vessels that escaped rowed direct to the Piræus to carry the terrible tidings. It arrived at night, and a sadder night was never known in Athens. The news spread through the city. Every house became a house of mourning. Nobody slept. All feared that Lysander would sail into the harbor with his victorious fleet. This was exactly what he did. All the seaports of Athens were blockaded by the Spartan vessels. The wheat supply was cut off, so that the people of the city were soon half starving.

The Athenians had now neither army nor fleet. After a three months' siege, during part of which time there was a severe famine, the city surrendered.

The only hope of the citizens was that their conquerors might be generous. But in this they were disappointed. The Spartans' terms were hard and cruel. One mile of each of the Long Walls was to be pulled down. Athens was to have no larger fleet than twelve ships of war. The Spartans were to name her rulers.

To wound the pride of Athens as much as possible Lysander

had the long walls pulled down to the sound of music, and a part of the work was done on the anniversary of the battle of Salamis, a day always celebrated in Athens in memory of her great victory over the Persians.

The Greek World during the Persian Wars (500–479 BC)

Thus ended the Peloponnesian War (404 B.C.). It had been a fierce struggle, and all Greece had suffered. Thucydides, who wrote the history of this war, says that never had so many cities been made desolate, never had there been such scenes of slaughter.

Athens was ruined. She had lost her ships and her army, and she was helpless in the hands of Sparta. Thirty men were appointed by the Spartans to govern the city. They are known in history as the "Thirty Tyrants." Their rule was very harsh.

They allowed only 3,000 Athenians to live in Athens. The rest of the people had to leave the city, and Sparta forbade all other Grecian cities to give them refuge. Thebes and Argos, however, boldly defied this cruel order, and many of the banished Athenians went to live in these cities.

After eight months the Athenians, under a leader named Thrasybulus, overthrew the "Tyrants." But in that short time no less than fourteen hundred Athenians citizens had been put to death.

Lysander's capture of Athens made him so popular in Sparta that for some years he was the real head of the government, and he made up his mind to seize the throne.

Before he could carry out his plans, however, he was put at the head of a Spartan force and sent to the city of Thebes, against which the Spartans had declared war. His army was routed by the Thebans and Lysander himself was among the slain.

Demosthenes

I

IN the city of Athens about twenty-five years after the Peloponnesian War there lived a delicate boy named Demosthenes. His father was a manufacturer of swords and made a great deal of money. But when Demosthenes was only seven years old his father died. Guardians had charge of his property for ten years. They robbed the boy of part of his fortune and managed the rest so badly that Demosthenes could not go to school to the best teachers in Athens because he had not money enough to pay them.

One day, when he was sixteen years old, a great trial was going on at Athens and he strolled into the court. There were fifteen hundred and one dicasts or, as we call them, jurymen in their seats, and the court was crowded with citizens who, like Demosthenes, had gone in from curiosity. A lawyer named Callistratus was speaking. He did not finish his speech for nearly four hours. But no one left the court until he ceased to speak. Then hundreds of people went out and hurried home. Demosthenes waited to see the end. When each of the jurymen had thrown a voting pebble into a basket the clerk of the court counted the pebbles and told the result. Callistratus had won the case.

Demosthenes went home determined to become a lawyer and public speaker. In one year from that time he brought suit against his guardians, delivered four orations against them and won his case. He recovered a large part of the property which his father had left to his mother and himself.

After this he entered public life, but the first time he made a speech in the public assembly it was a complete failure. He stammered and could not speak loud enough, and in trying to do so he made odd faces.

People laughed at him, and even his friends told him that he never could be a speaker, so he went home greatly cast down.

Then an actor who was a great friend of his family went to

see him and encouraged him. He asked Demosthenes to read to him some passages of poetry. Then the actor recited the same passages. The verses now seemed to have new meaning and beauty. The actor pronounced the words as if he felt them. The tones of his voice were clear and pleasant and his gestures were graceful. Demosthenes was charmed.

"You can learn to speak just as well as I do," said the actor, "if you are willing to work patiently. Do not be discouraged, but conquer your difficulties."

"I will," said Demosthenes. And he did.

It is said that to improve his voice he spoke with stones in his mouth, and to become accustomed to the noise and confusion of the public assembly he went to the seashore and recited there amid the roar of the waves. To overcome his habit of lifting one shoulder above the other he suspended a sword so that the point would prick his shoulder as he raised it.

He built an underground room in which he could study without interruption and practice speaking without disturbing any one. He had one side of his head shaved so that he would be ashamed to leave this retreat. Then he remained there for months at a time engaged in study. One thing that he did while there was to copy eight times the speeches in the famous history of Thucydides. This was to teach him to use the most fitting language. Besides all this he took lessons of an excellent speaker named Isæus who taught declamation. In this way the awkward boy who had been laughed out of the assembly became in time the greatest orator of Athens.

Not only was Demosthenes a graceful orator, but he was wise and patriotic. He soon acquired great influence in Athens and became one of the ten official orators.

At this time Philip of Macedon had organized a strong army and was beginning those conquests which in the end made him master of Greece. Demosthenes from the first regarded him with suspicion, but said nothing until convinced that Philip was threatening the liberty of Athens and of all Greece. Then he urged the Athenians to fight against Philip as their forefathers had fought against the Persians at Marathon, at Salamis and at Platæa. "Philip," he said, "is weak because he is selfish and unjust. He is strong only because he is energetic. Let us be equally energetic, and being unselfish and just, we shall triumph."

Philip's victory at Chæronea completely disheartened the Athenians, and Demosthenes had to use all the power of his eloquence to rouse them. In his speeches he showed how the success of Philip and the failure of Athens were not due to the advisers of the people or to the generals who led their army, but to the Athenians themselves. "You idle away your time," said he, "going into barbers' shops and asking what news to-day, while Philip is gathering forces with which to crush you and the rest of Greece with you."

Philip tried to bribe Demosthenes, but the orator was absolutely incorruptible, and to the end of his life he raised his voice and used his influence for the cause of freedom against both Philip and Alexander. He delivered twelve orations on this subject. Three of these orations were specially directed against Philip and are known as the "Philippics." They are so bitter in their denunciation of Philip that to-day any speech which is very bitter and severe against a man or a party is called a "Philippic."

The most famous speech that Demosthenes ever made was in defence of himself and is known as the speech "On the Crown." He had advised the Athenians to unite with the Thebans against Philip. His advice was followed, and a victory was won. The Athenians were so much pleased that it was proposed to crown Demosthenes with a golden wreath at one of the great festivals. Now this proposal had to be voted on by the people, and some of Demosthenes' enemies objected. If the people refused to vote the crown it would have meant disgrace for Demosthenes and so he was obliged to go before the assembly to speak in defense of himself and to show that his advice to his countrymen had been correct. It was true that the Athenians had not been able to destroy Philip's power, or free the states of Greece from his control; but, said Demosthenes, "I insist that even if it had been known beforehand to all the world that Philip would succeed and that we should fail, not even then ought Athens to have taken any other course if she had any regard for her own glory or for her past or for the ages to come." By this he meant that it was the duty of her people to fight for what they believed to be right even if in the very beginning they had known that they could not succeed.

Grander words than these never fell from human lips, and when the vote was taken the people decided that he should receive the crown.

II

WHEN news reached Athens of the murder of Philip,

Demosthenes rejoiced and placed a wreath upon his head, as if he were at a feast. He even persuaded the Athenians to make a thank-offering to their gods.

Alexander soon placed the Greek cities at his mercy. Then he demanded that Demosthenes and eight other Athenian orators should be delivered up to be punished for treason. Demosthenes told the people of Athens the story of the wolf and the sheep.

"Once on a time," he said, "the shepherds agreed with the wolf that henceforth they should be friends. The wolf promised faithfully never again to attack the sheep. But he said he thought it would be only fair that the shepherds should cease to keep dogs. The shepherds agreed and gave up their dogs. Then the wolf ate up the sheep."

The Athenians knew what Demosthenes meant, and heeded the lesson. They kept their watchdogs, Demosthenes and the other orators, safely at home.

Alexander at length withdrew his demand and treated the Athenians with kindness. However, this did not win the favor of Demosthenes, who continued to oppose the Macedonians at every step.

After some years one of Alexander's satraps stole a large treasure, fled to Athens and begged for protection. Demosthenes was unjustly accused of helping him and was condemned to pay a fine. He could not pay it and so went into exile.

When Alexander died the orator returned to Athens. The Athenians sent a man-of war to bring him to the Piræus. The magistrates, the priests and all the citizens marched out to welcome him and escort him to the city.

Demosthenes now made a last effort to free Athens. But Macedonia was still strong, and Athens and those who loved her were weak. In a short time the demand was again made that the orators be given up to be punished and Demosthenes again had to flee for his life. He sought refuge in a temple of Poseidon on an island near the coast of Greece.

The sacredness of the temple ought to have protected him, but he was not allowed to escape. The captain of the soldiers who were sent to kill him told him that if he would come out of the temple he should be pardoned. Demosthenes knew well that this promise would be broken. He asked to be allowed a few moments in which to write a letter, and his request was granted. He wrote, and then placed the end of his writing-quill in his mouth. Those who were watching saw him grow pale. He tried to reach the door, but fell dead near the altar. He had taken poison which he had long carried in the end of his writing-quill, for he feared that if he ever fell into the hands of the Macedonians, he would die in prison, or by torture.

Ptolemy

I

ONE of Alexander's favorite generals was Ptolemy. In the division of the Empire Egypt was placed in his charge. Other parts of the Empire were entrusted to other generals. One had Macedonia, another Thrace, another Syria. At first they ruled as governors for Alexander's young son, but after a while they became independent and were called kings.

Ptolemy and his descendants ruled Egypt for more than three hundred and fifty years. They were a great line of sovereigns and did much for the good of the country. We are accustomed to think of them as Egyptians, but really they were Greeks living in Egypt.

One of Ptolemy's first acts, and one which shows that he was a man of affectionate feeling, was to bring the body of Alexander from Babylon to Egypt. It was first buried in Memphis but afterward removed to Alexandria, because, as you remember, this city was founded by Alexander and named after him.

Ptolemy made Alexandria his capital and did a great deal to beautify the city. He founded a museum and began collecting books for a library.

His son, Ptolemy Philadelphus, carried on this work and made the library the largest and best in the world. Most of the books were made of the pith of the papyrus or paper plant, of which you have read in the story of Pisistratus. They were written in Greek and Latin.

Ptolemy appreciated the intelligence and learning of the Jews and treated them with so much kindness and gave them so many liberties that great numbers of them settled in Egypt.

Two things that Ptolemy Philadelphus did are especially worth remembering. One was to cause the Bible of the Jews to be translated into Greek; the other was to open again a great canal which had been dug many centuries before from the Nile to the Red Sea, but had long been filled up by the drifting sand of the desert. This was something like the cutting of the Suez Canal.

Ptolemy's canal connected the Atlantic with the Indian Ocean. Ships could sail from the Atlantic across the Mediterranean, then through the canal and the Red Sea, and on to India.

At that time Egypt raised more wheat than any other country in the world, so she had a great commerce. In exchange for her wheat she bought the products of Europe and Asia, and Alexandria became the richest city of the world.

But, more than that, the Ptolemies, especially Philadelphus, invited learned men to their court and gave them support so that they might carry on their own studies and teach others.

At one time there were 14,000 students receiving instruction in the city. Thus Alexandria became the home of learning. It was there that pupils were first taught that the earth is round, and one of the great astronomers who lived there found out very nearly the length of the earth's circumference and diameter.

The people of Alexandria knew more about these things two hundred years before Christ than the people of Europe did a thousand years after. The science of to-day about which you hear so much is only the continuation of what was begun by the wonderful Greeks whom the Ptolemies gathered about them in Alexandria.

One of the Ptolemy line was the celebrated Cleopatra, an able ruler and the most fascinating woman of her time. You will be able read something of her history in "The Famous Men of Rome."

Rome Rules the World

Our story began in Egypt and in the Valley of the Two Rivers. From there, civilization moved on to Greece. Now we shall see how civilization spread to other lands.

When you look at the map, you will see that Italy looks like a boot sticking out into the Mediterranean Sea. Like Greece, Italy is surrounded on three sides by the sea. Halfway down the boot, near the west coast, is the city of Rome. Because they lived near the center of Italy, the Romans were able to go on and conquer all the lands surrounding this important sea. The Romans became masters of what was then the known world.

In ancient times, the civilized people lived to the east of Italy. These were the Egyptians, the Phoenicians, the Hebrews, the Persians, and the Greeks. Most of the people who lived to the west of Italy were not civilized. Rome conquered both the civilized east and the uncivilized west. The Romans passed on the civilizations of the eastern lands to many of the wild tribes of the west. Many years later, some of these tribes overran the countries of Western Europe. Centuries later, these countries were to bring their civilizations to America.

The Romans were an important link between the world's oldest civilizations and our modern civilization.

Early Rome

There were three important groups of people living in Italy.
About 500 B.C., there were three important groups of people living in Italy. These were the Greeks in southern Italy, the

Etruscans in the north, and the Latin tribes between them.

The Greeks had established colonies in southern Italy and in Sicily. These colonies were like the cities of Greece. The people built temples with large columns, and many beautiful statues. They had their theaters and their schools. In other words, Greek civilization had spread to southern Italy.

The Etruscans lived in the northern part of Italy. The Etruscans are a mystery to us. We do not know exactly where they came from or how they became civilized. They worked in metals and made pottery. They lived in cities and had large buildings. They could read and write, but we have not yet found out how to read their writings.

Between these civilized Greeks and civilized Etruscans lived the Latin tribes. The Latins were not very civilized. They could not read or write or make beautiful things. They lived in crude houses and kept small farms.

The Latins had built a city overlooking the Tiber River about fifteen miles from the sea. This was the city of Rome. In 500 B.C., Rome was a city of crude houses and dirt streets. In that year no one would have thought that the Latins who lived in Rome would some day rule the world.

The Romans learned from their neighbors. Although the Romans (the name by which the Latins of Rome were known) were not very civilized at first, they learned the ways of civilization from their neighbors. From the Etruscans, they learned how to work with metal. The Etruscans also taught them how to organize an army.

Some of the Greeks from southern Italy sailed up the

Tiber River to trade with the Romans. From these Greek traders the Romans learned how to use coins. The Greeks also taught the Romans how to build ships. One of the most important things the Greeks taught the Romans was the alphabet. The Romans used the letters of the alphabet not only to write but to count. You have probably learned the Roman numerals.

The traders told the Romans about the gods that were worshiped in Greece. The Romans began to worship the same gods. They gave different names to the gods, however. The Greeks called their chief god Zeus, and the Romans called him Jupiter.

Rome becomes a republic. According to an old legend, Rome was ruled for 250 years by Etruscan kings. The legend says that one of these later kings was so cruel that the people drove him from the city.

We do not know whether or not the legend is true. We do know that in 509 B.C. the Romans set up a new kind of government. This government was a republic.

In forming their republic the Romans did not want any man to have too much power over them. At the head of the government there was not one man, but two men. These men were called consuls. One consul could not do anything unless he asked the other. Thus, each consul was a check upon the other one. The consuls were elected by the free men of Rome. If the Romans did not like what the consuls did, they could elect new consuls at the end of the year.

The Romans also had a Senate. The Senate had 300 members. They were called senators. The senators were elected by the people. We must remember, however, that only a small number of Romans were allowed to vote.

The senators who were elected advised the consuls and helped them rule.

When people rule themselves they have a democracy. Athens was a democracy the Roman Republic was a democracy, too, but it was different from Athens.

In Athens, the free men gathered together and made their own laws. In Rome, the free men elected certain men who made their laws for them.

Our United States is a republic. The voters elect the head of the government, and they elect the men who make the laws. Our government is different in many ways from the Roman Republic, but the idea of having a republic goes back to ancient Rome. Some of the words we use in government also come from Rome. We have a Senate, for example.

Dictators ruled in times of trouble. In time of war, the Romans needed someone who could act quickly. At such a time, the Senate elected a dictator. The dictator could rule as he thought best, and everybody had to obey him. At the end of six months, however, he had to give up his office.

The common people gain more power. When we read about Athens, we saw that it was not a perfect democ-racy. There were many people who were not allowed to vote or hold public office.

This was also true of Rome in the early days of the republic. The people were divided into two classes, the patricians and the plebeians. The patri-cians were the nobles, or the upper" class. They were descended from the people who had first founded Rome. The plebeians were the common people, or the lower class.

The patricians kept control of the government. They were the only ones allowed to vote. Only patricians and their descendants could become consuls or senators.

The plebeians complained that they were not being treated fairly. "We do all the hard work," they said. "We pay a large share of the taxes, and we do most of the fighting in time of war. Yet, we receive little in return. We are not allowed a voice in the government. We can be put in prison or sold as slaves if we are not able to pay our debts. We are not even allowed to marry patricians."

For a long time the patricians paid no attention to these complaints. Then the plebeians decided fo rebel. Many of them left the city and went to live on a nearby hill. The patricians saw that they could not get along without the plebeians. There was no one to do the hard work or to fight in the army. The patricians had to give in.

The plebeians were given the right to elect men called tribunes. If the senators tried to pass a law which the plebeians did not like, a tribune could stop them. He did this by shouting "Veto," which means "I forbid."

Little by little, the plebeians won more rights. They were allowed to marry patricians. Then a law was passed which said that at least one of the consuls had to be a plebeian. The plebeians won the right to vote. They also won the important right to become senators.

As the plebeians won more and more rights, Rome became more a government of the people. In other words, it became more democratic.

The laws are written. In the days when the patricians controlled Rome, there were no written laws. A patrician could say the law meant anything he. wished it to mean. The. patricians sometimes used the law to imprison plebeians and to take away their property.

When the common people gained more power, they said that the laws must be written down so that everyone would know what they were. The laws were carved on twelve large stone tablets. These tablets were set up in the market place, which was called the forum. Now, it was possible for everybody to know exactly what the laws said. School boys had to memorize the laws on the twelve tablets.

Check Your Knowledge

1. Why is the history of Rome important to us?
2. What did the Etruscans teach the Romans?
3. Name the things the Romans learned from the Greeks?
4. What do we call the new kind of government developed by the Romans?
5. Why were there two men at the head of the Roman government? What were these men called?
6. When did the Roman Senate elect a dictator?
7. To what two classes did the people of Rome belong?
8. Which class did the Roman tribunes represent?
9. How could the tribunes prevent the Senate from passing a law?

10. Why was it necessary to write down the Roman law.

Rome Conquers the World

The Romans unite all Italy. Rome was one of several city-states. In Italy, just at Athens was one of many city-states in Greece. Unlike the Greeks, however, the Romans were able to unite the peoples of Italy. Why were the Romans able to unite Italy, while the Greeks were not able to unite Greece? If you will look at a map of Italy you will see one very important reason. You remember that the mountains of Greece divided the

country into little sections. Now look at Italy, and see where the mountains are. To the north of Italy are the high mountains called the Alps. These mountains separate Italy from the rest of

Europe. In Italy, there is one large mountain range, the Apennines. These mountains run north and south and are near the Adriatic Sea. Between the mountains and the Mediterranean Sea there is a large region that is rather flat. This region has hills, such as the seven hills of Rome, but there are no high mountains. Most of the people of Italy lived in this flat section. It was easier for the people of Italy to unite simply because their country was not divided into little sections as Greece was.

When Rome was a city-state it was in danger from the other Latin tribes and from the Etruscans. The Romans saw that they had to conquer or be conquered. Roman armies went forth first to the nearby tribes and then to farther places. Some tribes and cities were willing to join Rome as friends and allies.

Others had to be conquered. By 265 B.C., all of Italy had come under Roman rule.

Most of the people in Italy were con-tent under Roman rule. The city-states had been fighting each other, and there had been much suffering and bloodshed. Now, the Romans brought an end to this fighting. The Romans also protected the people against enemies from outside. Italy. The people were still allowed to elect their own local chiefs and rulers.

Rome destroys Carthage. The Phoenicians founded the city of Carthage on the northern coast of Africa. At first, Carthage was a city-state but, like Rome, Carthage extended its rule farther and farther. Soon the Carthaginians held land on both sides of the Mediterranean Sea, as the map shows. They also held the islands of Sardinia and Corsica, which are close to Italy. They held half of Sicily, which is the island south of Italy.

Carthage and Rome grew into the two most powerful cities in this part of the world. They became great rivals. Rome fought three wars with Carthage. These are called the Punic Wars. The wars began in 264 B. C. In the first war the Romans drove the Carthaginians from the island of Sicily. When the war was over, the people of Sardinia and Corsica revolted against Carthage. All three islands then became Roman territory.

A great general fought in the second Punic War. He was Hannibal, the Carthaginian. Hannibal formed a large army in Spain. He had 50,000 foot soldiers, 9,000 horsemen, and 37 elephants. Hannibal led this army across Spain and France and then across the snow-covered Alps into Italy. Only a very great leader could have done this. The Romans were amazed and frightened when they heard that Hannibal was in Italy. He remained there for sixteen years. At one time he brought his men to the gates of Rome. He was never able to capture Rome, however.

Meanwhile, Roman soldiers were fighting in North Africa. The city of Carthage was in danger. Hannibal was called home to protect the city but he was not able to save it. The Romans captured Carthage, and the war was over. Carthage gave up her possessions in Spain, and she lost most of her power.

There was peace for fifty-three years. Then war broke out

again. This time the Romans destroyed the city of Carthage. They put salt on the ground where the city had been so that nothing would grow there. Rome took all the territory that had belonged to Carthage. All the land surrounding the western end of the Mediterranean Sea now belonged to Rome.

Rome becomes master of the Mediterranean. While Rome was fighting Carthage, she was also fighting countries at the eastern end of the Mediterranean. The Romans conquered Macedonia and Greece. They now ruled the land where the first great civilization of Europe had developed. The Romans conquered Egypt, the ancient land of the Pharaohs. They conquered Palestine and became the masters of God's chosen people, the Hebrews. In time Rome controlled the eastern end of the Mediterranean just as she did the western end.

We sometimes say that Rome ruled the world. We mean that she ruled most of the known world. At that time, the Mediterranean Sea was the most important body of water in the world. Nobody knew very much about the Atlantic Ocean or the other oceans. North America and South America would not be discovered until many centuries later. Most of Africa was a mystery. There were people living in India and China, but they were so far away and so difficult to reach that the Romans knew little about them. We see then that the Romans actually ruled most of the world that was known to them at that time.

There were two kinds of civilization in Roman lands. When the Romans conquered the eastern end of the Mediterranean they conquered people whose civilization was older than the civilization of the Romans. You remember that Alexander the

Great had spread Greek civilization throughout this region. Most of the people spoke Greek. They had Greek laws. They read Greek literature. They admired Greek statues. This part of the world kept its Greek civilization even after the Romans conquered it.

At the western end of the Mediterranean the Romans destroyed Carthage and its civilization. The Roman, or Latin, civilization spread through this region. In North Africa, Italy, Spain, and later in France and England the people spoke the Latin language. The more educated people read Latin literature. Their buildings looked like the buildings in Rome. This became the Latin part of the world.

We see, then, that there were two kinds of civilization in Roman lands: Latin civilization in the West and Greek civilization in the East.

Governors ruled the conquered lands. The Romans had secured self-government for themselves. They had also wisely given self-government to most of the other people of Italy. They were not so wise, however, in ruling the lands outside of Italy. The people in the lands ruled by Rome had almost nothing to say about their government.

The conquered land was divided into provinces. The Roman Senate appointed a governor to rule each province. The governor had as much power as if he had been a king. He brought his own officials with him from Rome and he had an army to see that his orders were carried out.

Many of the governors were cruel and greedy. They forced people to pay high taxes. Some governors robbed the people of their treasures and sent these treasures back to Rome. Not all the governors were bad, of course. But even when the governor tried to be just, the people of a province did not like to be ruled by someone who came from another country. **There were many good things about Roman rule**. Even though Roman rule had its faults, the Romans did many good things for the people in the provinces. Some sincere Romans even tried to undo the harm done by the evil governors.

Before these lands had been conquered by the Romans, their people had often fought bitter wars with each other. Some were overrun by savage tribes that raided cities and farms. In others, fierce robbers terrorized the people.

The Romans did not allow one province to fight with another, and in this way they brought peace to most of the world. They built paved roads throughout the provinces so that Roman armies could travel over them swiftly, and put down any trouble. These roads were also used by travelers, so that there was much travel in the Roman world.

A traveler could go over thousands of miles of well-paved roads in Roman lands. If he knew two languages, Latin and Greek, he could be understood almost everywhere he went. In all that distance he would never be in danger of being captured by savage tribesmen. He would probably never be bothered by robbers. He would never come to a country that was at war.

Check Your Knowledge

1. How did the geography of Italy help it to be a united country?

2. What is the name of Italy's one large mountain range?

3. Give three reasons why the people of Italy were happy under Roman rule.

4. What two islands near Italy were held by Carthage?

5. What were the wars between Carthage and Rome called?

6. What do we mean when we say that Rome ruled the world?

7. What were the two kinds of civilization in Roman lands?

8. In what lands outside of Rome was Latin spoken?

9. How were the conquered peoples out-side of Rome ruled?

10. How did the Romans bring peace to the world?

Romans Lose Their Self-Government

Life in Rome begins to change. Early Rome was a city of farmers. Almost all the people made their living by farming or by raising sheep. Cows, sheep, ducks, and geese often walked through the dirt streets. The people worked hard all day long. They lived in crudely built houses with dirt floors. They had little beauty in their lives.

Life began to change for the Romans when they became the rulers of all Italy. Life changed even more when they became the rulers of the world.

All the lands that were ruled by Rome were taxed; therefore, great amounts of money poured into Rome. Much of this money was used to erect new public buildings. Many of the streets were paved. When the Roman soldiers conquered the Greek cities they brought many Greek statues to Rome. These statues were placed in the public squares and public buildings.

There was also a great change in the way people made

their living. The Romans built paved roads through most of their lands. Almost all these roads ended at Rome. "All roads lead to Rome" was a common saying. People in other parts of the world used these roads to travel to Rome. Many Romans made their living buying and selling to these visitors. These Romans became merchants. Some plebeian families who had become powerful joined with the patricians to form a group called "the new nobility." Members of the new nobility sought out' public office, and the number of public officials increased.

The merchants and public officials did not have to work all day as the farmers did. They had more time to enjoy life. The Romans built theaters like the ones in Greece. They read Greek poetry and history. They talked about the ideas of the great Greek thinkers.

Rome had changed greatly since the days when it was a little farming village. Now it was a large city with paved streets and large public buildings and beautiful monuments.

Some people became very wealthy. As Rome became more and more powerful, some of her people became wealthy. Merchants made a great deal of money by selling supplies to the army in time of war. Army officers brought back many treasures from the provinces.

The rich people built magnificent houses. These houses had baths which were almost as large as our swimming pools. Public baths, which were actually clubs, attracted many Romans. The water in them was usually heated. Rich Romans spent hours in these warm baths. They had slaves to do all their work. When they traveled, they were carried in litters by slaves, or they rode in chariots.

The wealthy Romans enjoyed many pleasures and did little work to make up for their hours of play. They became soft and lazy. Most of them did not come by their wealth honestly. They grew more and more evil.

Most Romans were very poor. Some of the wealthy Romans owned large farms. They had many slaves on these farms. The slaves plowed the fields, and took care of the crops. They did all the other work on the farm.

The men who owned small farms did not own any slaves. They had to do all the work themselves. They had to charge higher prices for their grain and fruit. They found it difficult to make a living. Many of them had to sell their farms to the rich landowners.

A man who had to sell his farm usually took his family into the city. When he got there he found that it was almost impossible to find work. Most of the work which had once been done by free men was now done by slaves.

Soon there were thousands of poor families in Rome. They lived in miserable dwellings. When they could not find work they begged.

The people are given free bread and free entertainment. As the slaves continued to replace the free workers, the wealthy slave-owners grew concerned. They were afraid that the poor people of Rome would begin to envy the easy lives of the rich. They knew that this would lead to serious trouble.

The wealthy and powerful men of Rome began to give free bread to the poor people. Then, they decided that this was not enough and they began to provide free entertainment. The people gathered in places called amphitheaters. An amphitheater looks very much like a football stadium. The shows held in the amphitheaters were very cruel. Sometimes two athletes, called gladiators, would fight each other. Usually the fight went on until one of the gladiators was killed. Sometimes people from the conquered countries were brought in to fight lions, tigers, and other wild animals. These people were usually killed by the animals.

The common people became so accustomed to receiving free bread and free entertainment that they began to think that they had a right to these things. Some men even refused to work when they had a chance. "Work is for slaves," they said. "We are free Roman citizens and do not have work."

We can see that something had happened to the Romans since the days when they had been hard-working farmers. They had become lazy. This was true of both the rich Romans and the poor ones.

The people sell their votes. The politicians of Rome saw opportunity for themselves in the people's desire for free bread and free entertainment. They spent large sums of money feeding and entertaining the poor. In return, they asked the people to vote for them.

In a democracy it is important that the people think carefully before they vote. They should learn as much as possible about the men who are running for office. They should vote for the man they think will give them the best government.

The Romans no longer did this. They voted for the man

who provided the best entertainment. As a result, many unworthy men were elected to office. These men took bribes and stole money that belonged to the government. The people did not seem to care.

Many years before, the common people of Rome had struggled hard to gain a voice in the government. Now their descendants were selling their votes for bread and entertainment.

The Gracchi brothers try to help the people. There were some men in Rome who were very much worried about the way things were going. They thought that the idea of free bread and free entertainment was bad for the country as well as for the people. They believed that everyone should have the chance to earn a living.

Two of the men who felt this way were the brothers Tiberius and Gaius Gracchus. Tiberius became a tribune. He had a law passed which would provide small farms for the men who had no work. Many Romans were opposed to this law. There were riots and fights in the streets. Tiberius lost his life before his law could go into effect. Gaius Gracchus tried to carry out his brother's program. Gaius also wished the government to build roads and public buildings in order to provide jobs for those who had no work. Gains, too, lost his life.

When people are not able to rule themselves, they soon have someone ruling them. This happened in Rome. A general named Sulla had himself appointed "Permanent Dictator." This meant that he did not have to give up his office at the end of six months as all the previous dictators had done. Sulla ruled as he pleased and paid little attention to the Senate. Self-government in Rome was coming to an end.

Julius Caesar becomes ruler of Rome. Julius Caesar was born in Rome about 100 years before the birth of Our Lord.

He was very popular with the people, and he was elected to many offices. He provided many free shows, as did other men who wished to be elected. However, he was more honest and fair than most of the men elected to office in this way.

Caesar was made governor of the Roman province of Iberia, now known as Spain. North of his province was the country which was then known as Gaul. Today, we call it France. The Gauls were fierce fighters and had never been conquered by the Romans. Caesar feared they planned to attack his province. He decided to conquer them. The war against the Gauls lasted for many years. Caesar was victorious and Gaul became a Roman province.

Caesar became even more popular with the people of Rome when they learned that he had conquered the Gauls. Some of the senators thought that Caesar was becoming too popular. They ordered him to leave his army and come back to Rome. Because Caesar· feared that his enemies in Rome might kill him or put him in prison, he took his army to Rome with him. He led his army to the edge of his province. The boundary of the province was a little stream called the Rubicon. He led his army across the Rubicon.

He had disobeyed the Senate. Now he could not turn back. Today when someone makes a very important decision from which he cannot turn back we say, "He has crossed the

Rubicon."

First Caesar defeated his enemies in Rome, and then he defeated his enemies in the provinces. After that, the Senate appointed him dictator for life. Caesar had absolute power over Rome and all the lands ruled by Rome.

Caesar proved to be a good ruler. If the Romans had to be ruled by a dictator, Julius Caesar was probably the best man for the job. He proved to be a wise and just ruler. He set about making the government better and making things better for the people. He insisted that the governors treat the provinces justly. He gave land to needy families. He lowered taxes. He planned to send many poor Roman families to the provinces where they could make a new start in life. He erected many new public buildings which would improve Rome and also give work to the jobless. He reduced the number of people who were fed by the government. Julius Caesar introduced the Egyptian calendar into Rome after he made some changes in it. He introduced the idea of leap year an extra day every four years. He named one of the months, July, for himself.

Caesar is murdered. Julius Caesar did not have time to do all the things he wished. One day when he entered the Senate chamber a group of men came up to him. They pretended that they wished to talk with him. Suddenly they drew their knives and stabbed him to death.

Why did these men kill Caesar? Some of them were his enemies;

they killed him because they wished to gain con-trol of Rome.

Strangely enough, some of the men who killed Caesar liked him, and thought he was a good ruler. These men believed in democracy and self-government. They did not like the idea of having a dictator. They thought that if they killed Caesar the people would again control the government.

These men were mistaken. The people had become so selfish and lazy that they were no longer able to rule themselves. They never regained their self-government. The government had become weak and could not take on the task of ruling so large an empire.

Check Your Knowledge

I. How did most of the people of early Rome make their living?

2. When did life begin to change for the Romans?

3. Whose ideas did the Romans talk about?

4. In what ways did some Romans become very rich?

5. Why did many Roman farmers have to give up their farms?

6. Why were free bread and entertainment given to the common people?

7. Who tried to give the Roman people the biggest shows?

8. What happens when people can no longer rule themselves?

9. Why did the Romans decide to conquer Gaul?

10. What did Caesar do to help the common people of Rome?

The Beginning of the Roman Empire

Augustus Caesar becomes ruler of Rome. Octavius was the nephew of Julius Caesar and also his adopted son. In his will

Julius Caesar ordered that Octavius should succeed him as ruler of the Roman world. Octavius was only eighteen years old when Caesar died. For a time he ruled with two other men. In the year 31 B.C., Octavius became the ruler of Rome.

Octavius knew that the Romans did not want their government to be changed. He made no attempt to have himself called a king. However, the Senate gave Octavius the name Augustus, which means "honored." Before this the word had been used only for the gods. Octavius liked the name and used it all the time. We call him the Emperor Augustus. Under his rule, the Roman Republic came to an end and Augustus was, in fact, the first ruler of the Roman Empire. Augustus ruled wisely and the people of Rome scarcely realized that their republic had come to an end.

Augustus rules a well-ordered empire. Augustus reigned for forty years. Under him, Rome had its golden age.

Under Augustus and the emperors who followed him, the civilized world enjoyed almost complete peace. This was called the Pax Romana or "Roman Peace." It was during this time that Roman and Greek civilization spread among the people of Europe. The magnificent Roman roads kept the people of the empire in touch with each other all the way into Asia Minor. People were able to exchange ideas on almost every subject. This helped them to improve their way of living.

Since Augustus had no wars to fight, he could give all his time to improving the city and the empire. In Rome, Augustus organized a police department and a fire department. Many new public buildings were erected. In their architecture, the

Romans used the Greek columns and the arch which had been developed by the Etruscans. An arch is usually built of brick or stone. It has two upright sides which meet in a rounded peak. The Romans learned that they could build four arches and put a curved roof over them to form a dome. We still use the Roman arch and dome in many of our present-day buildings.

The buildings which were erected during the time of Augustus were of beautiful marble. The emperor once said of Rome: "I found it brick and left it marble."

Augustus put an end to idleness. Men who were strong and healthy could earn their living by working on the new buildings. If they did not accept this offer, they went hungry. Free bread was given only to the sick, the crippled, and the weak.

Many famous writers lived about the time of Augustus. Cicero was a famous prose writer. Virgil and Horace wrote beautiful poetry. There were some fine historians who lived at this time also.

Augustus and Rome were famous for many things. There is one thing, however, for which both are remembered above all others. It was while Augustus ruled the world that Our Lord was born in the stable at Bethlehem. It was during the *Pax Romana* that Christianity gradually spread throughout the empire.

Check Your Knowledge

I. When did Octavius become the ruler of Rome?

2. What does Augustus mean?

3. How did Augustus put an end to idleness in Rome?

4. What is meant by the Pax Romana?

5. For what event above all others do we remember Augustus?

Our Lord Founds His Church

When the Roman Empire was at its height, Jesus Christ, Son of God, came upon earth. By His life, suffering and death, Our Lord reopened for us the gates of Heaven which had been closed since the sin of our first parents. By His Resurrection especially Our Lord proved that He was really God.

While on earth, Our Lord established His Church, the Roman Catholic Church. Through the Church, Christ is still in the world and gives us a new way to live. The teachings of Our Lord and His Church have changed the whole story of mankind and will continue to do so until the end of the world.

In this Chapter, we shall read about Our Lord's life on this earth and about the first three centuries of His Church.

The Coming of the Redeemer

The Hebrews are conquered by the Romans. The Romans conquered Palestine in 63 B.C. The Hebrews, God's Chosen People, were now put under the rule of a Roman governor. Like many other conquered people, the Hebrews were not happy. They longed to be free of Roman rule.

The Hebrews knew that God had promised them a Redeemer. He had made this promise to Abraham. He also sent prophets to remind the Hebrews that a Redeemer would come. The Hebrews, however, failed to understand the prophecies about the Redeemer. They thought that He would save them from Roman rule. "We are not very happy now," the Hebrews sometimes said to each other, "but when the Redeemer comes, He will be a great king. He will make us an independent nation, as we were in the days of King David and King Solomon. They did not understand that the Redeemer was to be the King of Heaven and not an earthly king.

God becomes man. You have read the story about the birth of Our Lord. You know that the Angel Gabriel announced to Mary, the Hebrew girl, that she was to be the Mother of the

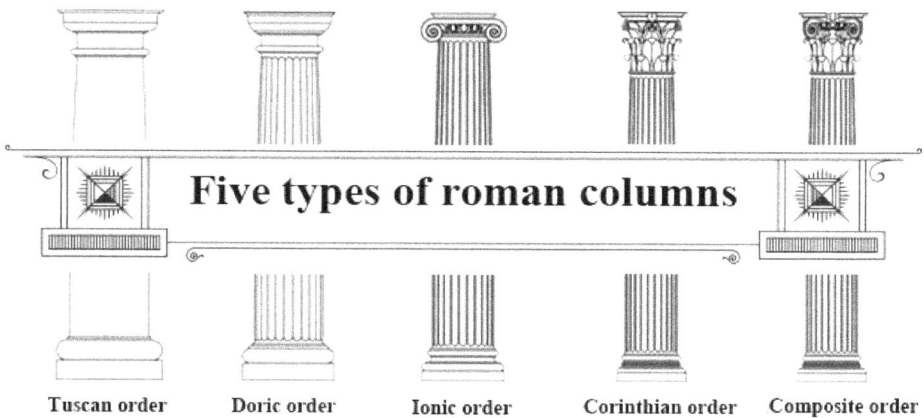

Five types of roman columns

Tuscan order   Doric order   Ionic order   Corinthian order   Composite order

Redeemer. Mary was a descendant of King David. So was Joseph, the foster father of Jesus. Many years before, God had told King David that the Redeemer would be descended from him.

In the last chapter, we read about Augustus, the first Roman emperor. Augustus wished to find out how many people lived in his empire. When a government counts its people we say it is taking a census. Today, when there is a census, somebody comes to our door and asks how many people live in the house Augustus did not do it this way. All the people were required to go to the home of their ancestors to be counted. Therefore, Mary and Joseph had to go to Bethlehem, the birthplace of King David.

The prophets had said that the Redeemer would be born in Bethlehem. Augustus did not know it, but he was helping to carry out God's plan when he ordered the census to be taken.

You know the rest of the story. You know that Jesus was born in a stable because there was no room in the inn. Thus the promised Redeemer came into the world.

Jesus lives in Nazareth. Jesus spent most of His life in Nazareth. We do not know very much about His boyhood. The Bible does tell us, however, that Jesus was "subject" to Mary and Joseph. This means that He obeyed them. He was God, and He had created the world, but He obeyed Mary and Joseph. We can also be certain that Jesus helped Joseph in the carpenter shop and that he helped Mary with the work about the house. The three gathered together to say their prayers. They made trips to the temple to offer sacrifices to God. They probably went for walks together and took part in simple amusements.

The Holy Family set the example which God wishes all families to follow.

Jesus preaches and teaches. When Jesus was about thirty years old, He began preaching and teaching. This was the beginning of His public life. Sometimes, to prove that He was really God, He worked miracles. He cured the sick and the blind. He even raised dead people to life.

Jesus preached love. Once He was asked which was the greatest commandment. He answered: "'Thou shalt love the

Lord thy God with thy whole heart, and with thy whole soul, and with thy whole mind.' This is the greatest and the first commandment. And the second is like it. 'Thou shalt love thy neighbor as thyself.'" All the other commandments are based on these two commandments. We must love God, and we must love all other human beings because God created them in His image and likeness.

Through His preaching and miracles, Jesus gained many followers among the Jews. The leaders of the Jews; however, hated Jesus. They feared that He was becoming too popular. They feared that they would lose their power if all the Jews turned to Jesus. These leaders - the Scribes and Pharisees - often tried to trap Jesus into saying something that would cause the people to turn against Him.

The Pharisees knew that the Jews hated to pay taxes to the Romans. They sent a group of people to ask Jesus whether they should pay taxes to the emperor. The Pharisees thought that Jesus would be in trouble no matter which way He answered. The Jews would not like it if Jesus said they should pay the taxes. The Romans would not like it if He said they should not pay the taxes.

As the Pharisees looked on, Jesus asked to see a coin. Then He asked whose picture was on the coin. The people answered, "Caesar's." Jesus said, "Render, therefore, to Caesar the things that are Caesar's, and to God the things that are God's."

The Pharisees had no answer to this, and they walked away. The answer which Jesus gave to the Pharisees is a very important one. It shows that we have duties toward God and duties toward our government: If our government is a good one we shall have no trouble obeying its laws while we are also obeying God's laws.

Jesus is put to death. The leaders of the Jews decided that the only way to keep Jesus from gaining followers was to put Him to death. As Roman subjects, however, they were not permitted to impose the death penalty. If they judged a person to be guilty of death, he was brought before the Roman governor who would pass the sentence. After many attempts to find some cause for death, the chief priests accused Jesus of blasphemy because He said that He was Christ, the Son of God.

The governor of the province of Judea, which included Palestine, was a Roman named Pontius Pilate. Pilate did not believe that Jesus deserved to be sentenced to death. He was a weak man, however, and he did not wish to have trouble with the Jewish leaders. When someone in the mob shouted that Jesus had even caused trouble in Galilee, Pilate sent Him to Herod, the king of Galilee. By doing this, he hoped to escape the responsibility of condemning Jesus. Herod, in turn, sent Jesus back to Pilate. Despite the fact that he still believed Jesus to be innocent' of the charges against Him, Pilate delivered Our Lord to the mob to be put to death.

Jesus was nailed to a cross, and there He died after terrible suffering. By His suffering and death He reopened for us the gates of Heaven. God's promise to mankind of a Redeemer had been fulfilled.

Jesus rises from the dead. Jesus was taken down from the cross, and His body was placed in the tomb. From Friday evening until Sunday morning Jesus lay in the tomb. On Sunday, the first Easter, He rose from the dead. In this way He proved that He was God. Only God can die and bring Himself back to life.

Jesus remained on earth for forty days after His Resurrection. During this time He prepared His followers for the task of spreading His teachings. He promised that He would send the Holy Ghost to guide them and to remain forever with His Church. After forty days He ascended into Heaven.

Check Your Knowledge

I. What nation ruled Palestine when Our Lord. was born?

2. Who reminded the Hebrews that a Redeemer would come?

3. What kind of king did the Hebrews expect the Redeemer to be?

4. How did Jesus live in Nazareth?

5. When did Jesus begin to preach and to teach?

6. What did Jesus often do to prove that He was God?

7. Name the two commandments upon which the other commandments depend.

8. Why did the Scribes and Pharisees try to trap Jesus?

9. How did Jesus reopen the gates of Heaven?

10. What did Jesus do during the forty days after He rose from the dead?

The Apostles Spread the Word of Our Lord

The Hebrews worshiped God according to the Old Law. For hundreds of years the Hebrews, or Jews, had believed in the One True God. They had the Ten Commandments and the other rules that God had given them. They worshiped God in the way He wished to be worshiped at that time. One of the ways in which the Hebrews wor-shiped God was to offer sacrifices. A lamb, or a goat, or an ox was brought into the temple and placed on a stone altar. Then it was killed and burned. While it was being burned the priests led the people in prayer.

The Hebrews worshiped God according to the Old Law. God Himself had given the Old Law to the Hebrews. Until Our Lord came on earth and gave us the New Law, the Hebrews had the one true religion.

Our Lord founds a new Church. When Our Lord was upon earth, He said that we were no longer to worship God according to the Old Law. He gave us a New Law. The New Law kept some parts of the Old Law, such as the Ten Commandments. Other parts were changed.

Our Lord gave us a new kind of sacrifice, a perfect sacrifice. This is the Holy Sacrifice of the Mass. Under the New Law we do not offer animals to God. We offer Our Lord Himself under the appearances of bread and wine.

Christ also gave us the seven sacraments to increase grace in our souls.

He gave us many other things, too. All these are in the Church He founded. In early days this was called the Christian Church.

Today it is called the Roman Catholic Church.

Under the Old Law, the Hebrew religion was the one true religion. Under the New Law the Catholic religion is the one true religion.

Our Lord chooses Apostles to carry on His work. Jesus chose twelve men to be the rulers of His Church and to carry on His work on earth. These were the twelve Apostles. One of the Apostles was named Simon. Our Lord told Simon that he was to be called Peter, which means rock. Our Lord said: "Thou art Peter, and upon this rock I will build My Church, and the gates of hell shall not prevail against it."

With these words He made Peter the head of the Church. At the Last Supper, the night before He died, Jesus offered the first Mass and gave His Apostles their first Holy Communion. At the same time, he ordained them as the first priests.

Just before He ascended into Heaven, Our Lord told the Apostles to teach His Word to all nations: "Go, therefore, and make disciples of all nations, baptizing them in the name of the Father, and of the Son, and of the Holy Spirit, teaching them to observe all that I have commanded you." This meant that they should convert people.

Then Jesus added: "And behold I am with you all days, even unto the consummation of the world." This was Our Lord's promise that He would always watch over the Church and that it would last until the end of the world. No persecution would ever be able to destroy it.

Our Lord knew that the Apostles were timid about preaching the new religion. He told them to wait in Jerusalem until the Holy Spirit came down upon them. While they waited, they chose Matthias to be the twelfth Apostle. He took the place of Judas who had betrayed Jesus to His enemies.

Ten days after Our Lord ascended into Heaven, the Holy Spirit came down upon the Apostles while they were at prayer. They were now filled with courage and understanding. They began to praise God in languages they had not known before. They were ready to begin their preaching. The descent of the Holy Ghost is commemorated on the Feast of Pentecost.

Saint Peter becomes Bishop of Rome. The Apostles traveled to many parts of the world. They were helped by the fact that most of the world belonged to the Roman Empire. They traveled over the roads the Romans had built through the empire. There were no wars to interfere with their work, because this was the time of the Roman Peace.

Every place the Apostles went they made converts. The number of Christians increased every day.

Saint Peter preached in many cities of the East, and then he went to Rome. He remained in Rome for the rest of his life. All the Apostles were bishops, and Saint Peter became the Bishop of Rome. Rome, as you know, was the most important city in the world at that time. It was the capital of the great Roman Empire.

Other Apostles went to other cities and became bishops of those cities. They all knew that Saint Peter was the head of the Church, because Our Lord had made him the head. After Saint Peter's death, Linus became the new Bishop of Rome and head of the Church because he was the successor of Saint Peter.

The Bishop of Rome has been the head of the Church ever since. We call him the Pope.

The Christians in Palestine are persecuted. Many of the first converts to the Christian religion were Jews. This is not surprising. The Jews believed in the One True God, and they knew that a Redeemer had been promised to the world. Many of them realized that Jesus was this promised Redeemer.

Most of the Jewish leaders, however, were opposed to Jesus. We know that they were always trying to trap Jesus into saying something that would make Him unpopular. Then they had Him put to death, and they thought that would be the last they would ever hear from Him. They soon realized their mistake. The Apostles preached in Jerusalem and in the other cities of Palestine. Thousands of Jews came into the Christian Church.

The Jewish leaders found that Jesus had more followers after His death than He had when He was alive. The leaders began to persecute the first Christians as they had persecuted Jesus Himself. The first persecutions of the Christians took place in Jerusalem.

The first Christian to give his life for his faith was a young man named Stephen. We call him the first martyr. He was stoned to death at Jerusalem because he would not give up his belief in the teachings of Our Lord. After Stephen, there were many more martyrs. The number of people who were coming into the Church, however, was greater than the number who were killed.

An enemy of the Church becomes its friend. A man named Saul of Tarsus watched with approval while Stephen was stoned to death. Saul was a Jewish leader who hated Christians. He thought it was his duty to put all Christians in prison.

One day Saul set out for Damascus. He heard that there were Christians in that city, and he wished to arrest them.

Suddenly Saul was surrounded by a light brighter than the sun. He was thrown to the ground. He heard a voice saying, "Saul, Saul, why dost thou persecute Me?"
Saul said, "Who art thou, Lord?" "I am Jesus of Nazareth whom thou art persecuting."

Saul found that he was blind. He made his way to Damascus. There he was baptized. He took the name Paul. He was able to see again as soon as he was baptized.
Paul now worked as hard to build up the Church as he had once worked to destroy it. He spent the next ten years preaching and teaching.

He traveled in the eastern, or Greek, part of the empire, and he spoke Greek very well. He founded many churches. While he was traveling he wrote letters to the people in these churches. These letters are the epistles of Saint Paul. Other Apostles also wrote epistles.
Saint Paul was not one of the twelve Apostles, but he is usually classed with them. He might be called the thirteenth Apostle. He is often called the "Apostle to the Gentiles," because he preached to people who were not Jews.

Saint Paul and all of the Apostles except John were martyrs. John was saved only by a miracle. He had been thrown into boiling oil but remained unharmed.
Jerusalem is destroyed. While Our Lord was on this earth, He

said that Jerusalem, the great city of the Jews, would be destroyed. This happened less than forty years after Our Lord's death. The Jews revolted against the Romans. The Romans sent a large army against Jerusalem. The Jews defended Jerusalem for a long time. There was great suffering in the city, because the people did not have enough to eat. Finally, the Romans were able to climb over the walls of Jerusalem. In the fighting, the city was destroyed.

Many of the Jews died in the fighting. Some fled to other parts of the world. The ones who stayed in Palestine became slaves. Palestine had once been the Promised Land of the Hebrews. Now, the Jews no longer had a land of their own.

Check Your Knowledge

I. What was the perfect sacrifice given in the New Law?

2. For what purpose were the twelve Apostles chosen?

3. What two things did Jesus do at the Last Supper?

4. Why did the Apostles have courage after Jesus ascended into Heaven?

5. Of what place was St. Peter the Bishop?

6. What helped the Apostles in traveling all over the world?

7. Where did the first persecution of the Church take place?

8. Why was St. Stephen stoned to death?

9. In which part of the Roman Empire did Paul travel the most?

10. What happened to Jerusalem almost forty years after the death of Our Lord?

The Christians in Rome

The Romans thought the Christians were their enemies. Our Lord lived and died in Palestine, far from Rome. The people of Rome did not hear about Christ until Saint Peter began to preach there. A few of the Romans became Christians when they heard Saint Peter preach. Most of the Romans, however, continued to be pagans.

What did the pagan Romans think of the Christians? At first, they thought that the Christians were a very strange people. Later they decided that the Christians were their enemies. From what we know about the Romans, we can see why they thought this way. The Christians seemed to preach against all the things the Romans liked best.

Many of the Romans were very cruel. We know that they flocked to their am-phitheaters in large numbers to watch the murder of helpless captives. The Christians reminded them that this was against God's law.

Wealthy Romans thought it was important to have large houses with many comforts. Some were lazy and looked down on work. They made slaves of the people their armies conquered and made them do the hard work. The

Christians taught that these abuses were wrong. They pointed out that worldly honor and possessions are not important. They said that Christ Himself had worked as a carpenter. They reminded the Romans that the slaves were also God's creatures and their equals in the eyes of God.

Christ's teachings appealed especially to the poor, the slaves, and the ill-treated Romans. The Christian religion gave them strength to bear their burdens in this world and to hope for the future in the next world. It was a religion of love and not one of fear and hate and slavery.

Perhaps the thing that made the Romans most angry with the Christians was their refusal to adore the pagan gods. To the Romans, this was a crime against the State. When the Christians also refused to worship the emperor, the Romans accused them of being traitors. Because certain groups of Romans despised the Christians, they spread many false rumors about them. All calamities such as earthquakes, floods, and serious illness were blamed on the Christians.

The Christians are persecuted. In July of the year 64 A.D., a fire destroyed a large part of Rome. Many of the Romans said that the emperor Nero had started the fire. They were very angry with the emperor. Nero was afraid the people might rise up against him. He accused the Christians of starting the fire. The pagan Romans were ready to believe this, because they did not like the Christians anyway.

This started a great persecution of the Christians. Some Christians were thrown to wild animals. Others were cruelly tortured until they died. Some were covered with oil and burned to light Nero's gardens. During this persecution by Nero, Saint Peter and Saint Paul were put to death. Saint Peter was crucified. He asked to be crucified upside down because he was not worthy to die as Our Lord had. Saint Paul was beheaded.

The next 250 years saw many persecutions of the Christians. Some were in Rome while others spread throughout the empire.

The Christians went to their death with great courage. Some even sang hymns as they were marched off to die. Their courage impressed other people. "They must have the true religion if they are willing to die for it," people reasoned. Every time a Christian was killed, many more people were baptized. Far from putting an end to the Church, the persecutions only seemed to help it grow. This is what people mean when they say: "The blood of the martyrs is the seed of the Church."

The Christians meet in secret. How did the Christians attend Mass and receive Communion during the perse-cutions? Often they met in secret. Sometimes they met in the home of one of the Christians. When they did this, they had to be careful that the Roman soldiers did not see them.

A Roman law said that burial places were sacred and must not be disturbed. In the early persecutions, the Christians often met in the graveyards. Here no one was allowed to disturb them. Many of the burial places were located in tunnels under the city of Rome. These underground tunnels were called catacombs.

When a priest said Mass in a burial place, he sometimes used the slab containing the grave of a martyr as an altar. We have a reminder of this in our churches today. In each altar there is an altar stone. This stone contains relics of martyrs.

In the later persecutions, the Romans paid no attention to the law which said that burial places should not be disturbed. Christians were arrested even when they held their services in the graveyards or in the catacombs.

In spite of the persecutions, the Christians managed to

build churches throughout the empire. In the city of Rome alone there were about forty Christian churches in the year 314 A.D. These churches were very much like the homes of wealthy Romans.

Persecution comes to an end. A powerful Roman named Constantine was friendly toward the Christians. Constantine's mother was Saint Helena who found the True Cross. He himself became a Christian just before he died.

In the year 312 A.D. Constantine was waging war with a powerful rival. They were fighting to see which man would become emperor. Before an important battle Constantine and his men saw a cross in the sky. On the cross was written: "In this sign thou shalt conquer." Constantine immediately took the cross as his badge. Although his men were outnumbered three to one, Constantine won the battle. He became the emperor of Rome.

The following year, 313 A.D., Constantine issued a new law. This is called the Edict of Milan. The law said that the Christians were no longer to be persecuted. There was great rejoicing among the Christians.

Two and a half centuries of persecution had come to an end. Now the Christians were free to practice their religion openly and without fear.

Check Your Knowledge

1. When did the Romans first hear about Christ?
2. What made the Romans decide that the Christians were their enemies?

---

3. What made the Romans most angry at the Christians?

4. On whom did Nero lay the blame for the fire in Rome?

5. How were the Christians persecuted?

6. How was St. Peter slain?

7. What is meant by the saying, "The blood of the martyrs is the seed of the Church"?

8. Why did the early Christians meet in graveyards?

9. How did Constantine become the em-peror of Rome?

10. What law said that Christians must no longer be persecuted?

The Church and the Empire

After the Edict of Milan, it seemed that all would be well for the Church. It was not long, however, before the Church faced new enemies. Men who called themselves Christians taught false doctrines. Germanic tribes from northern Europe came into the Roman Empire in large numbers, leaving disorder and destruction in their path. The empire itself was coming to an end.

In this Chapter, we shall learn about the problems faced by the Church in the years between 313 A.D. and 496 A.D. We shall learn how great men of God protected His teachings. We shall learn how the Church began the task of converting the Germanic tribes, and took on the responsibility of safeguarding what was best in Greek and Roman civilization.

IXΘYC

The Church After the Persecutions

Constantine helps the Church. Constantine did more than stop the persecution of the Church. He helped the Church in many ways. He gave the Pope his own Lateran Palace. He built a church for the Pope near the palace. This was the Lateran Basilica. For hundreds of years after that the Popes lived at the Lateran Palace. This was before they moved to the Vatican.

Constantine also built a great church to house the tomb where Saint Peter was buried. This church was called St. Peter's. It was the largest church in the world for many years. It stood until more than a thousand years. The present St. Peter's is the second great church built on this site. Constantine is said to have worked on St. Peter's with his own hands. He is said to have carried twelve basketloads of earth in honor of the twelve Apostles.

The bishops meet at Nicaea. The Church was no longer persecuted, but it faced new problems. Certain Christians refused to believe all the truths taught by God's Church. A priest named Arius, for example, taught that Christ was not God. For teaching this error, he was excommunicated. This means that he was put out of the Church. Arius went right on teaching the error, however, and he won many followers. Men like Arius who are Christians but do not believe all the teachings of the Church are called heretics. The errors which they teach are called heresies.

With the approval of Pope Sylvester, Constantine called a meeting of the bishops of the Catholic Church. One of the principal purposes of the meet-ing was to discuss the heresy of

Arius. Constantine said that he considered heresy "more dreadful and more painful than any war."

The meeting was held at Nicaea in Asia Minor, in 325 A.D. It is called the Council of Nicaea. The bishops declared that Christ is God and that all Catholics must believe this truth. They drew up a list of Catholic beliefs. This developed later into what we call the Nicene Creed. This creed is read at Mass on Sundays and on great feasts. It is sung by the choir at High Mass.

Another thing the bishops did was to fix the date of Easter. Until then, Easter had been celebrated on different Sundays in various parts of the empire.

The Fathers of the Church explain the Christian religion.
When Constantine ended the persecution of the Church, only about one out of every ten people in the empire was a Catholic. This meant that nine out of ten people were still pagans. These pagans knew very little about the Christian religion.

Germans from northern Europe were moving into the empire. These Germans knew nothing about Our Lord's teachings. Many heretics were teaching wrong ideas about the Christian religion. The Church now needed great writers and thinkers who could explain he Christian religion and defend it against heretics. In every age, God raises up saints who are needed for that time. In the important years after the Edict of Milan, God raised up great saints called the Fathers of the Church. These men were brilliant thinkers and writers. The Church has also given certain of these Fathers the title of "Doctor of the Church." These saints received this honor because of their holiness and their skill in explaining Christian truths. Four of the Doctors of the Church lived in the eastern part of the empire. They wrote in Greek. They are called the Greek Doctors. They are Saint Athanasius, Saint Basil the Great, Saint Gregory Nazianzen, and Saint John Chrysostom. Chrysostom means "golden mouthed." Saint John was given that name because he was such a good preacher. There were also four Latin Doctors. They lived in the western part of the empire and wrote in Latin. They are Saint Gregory the Great, St. Ambrose, Saint Augustine, and Saint Gregory the Great was the Pope, but he found time to do much writing. Saint Ambrose was the Bishop of Milan in Italy. He is known for his books and also for the hymns which he wrote. Saint Jerome's greatest work was revising the Latin translation of the four Gospels. Besides this work, Saint Jerome completed, with the exception of a few books, a translation of the Old Testament from the Hebrew. Saint Jerome's version of the Old and the New Testaments is called the Latin Vulgate.

Saint Augustine was born in North Africa. His mother, Saint Monica, was a fine Christian woman. Augustine's father was a pagan and he did not permit the boy to be baptized. Augustine had a great mind, and he became a brilliant scholar, but he would not be a Catholic. His mother pleaded with him and she prayed for him. To get away from his mother's pleadings, Augustine went to Milan to become a teacher. There he met and was converted by Saint Ambrose. His mother's prayers had been answered after many years. Augustine became the Bishop of Hippo in North Africa. His best known writings are his Confessions and the City of God.

The writing of these great Doctors of the Church were read and studied throughout the civilized world. Non-Catholics who read them learned more about the Catholic Faith. Catholics who read them became stronger in the Faith. Later writers and scholars were helped by referring to these writings which are still widely read today.

The Catholic religion becomes the religion of the empire.
Constantine had ended the persecution of the Church. The emperor Theodosius the Great, who reigned from 379 to 395 A.D., went further. He made the Catholic religion the religion of the empire. The old pagan temples were closed. The feast days of the Church became holidays. At the beginning of the fourth century, Catholics were in fear of being put to death for their religion. At the end of the fourth century their religion was the religion of the empire.

We are told that there was one time when Theodosius did not act like a good Christian. Some people in Thessaly murdered their governor. In anger, Theodosius had all the people of the city put to death.

Saint Ambrose was the Bishop of Milan at that time. Ambrose told the emperor that he had committed a terrible crime. He said that the emperor must do penance. Theodosius realized that he had done wrong. He came to church as a humble penitent, without his frown or royal robes. He stood before a large crowd and said he was sorry for what he had done.

Theodosius was a mighty emperor with a great army. Ambrose was a Bishop with no army at all. Ambrose could not force the emperor to do penance. But the emperor knew that obeying the law of God was more important than anything else. He showed his sorrow by doing penance for his sins.

The Church borrowed many ideas from the Roman Empire. Today we still have many reminders that the Church had its beginning in the days of the Roman Empire. Our Mass, for example, is still said in Latin. In the middle of the fourth century, most of the people in the western part of the empire spoke Latin. They could understand all the prayers which the priest said at Mass.

You may have noticed that the vestments which priests wear today look somewhat like the clothes which the Romans wore. This is because the first vestments were like the clothes worn in the days of the Roman Empire.

You have learned that the Roman Empire was divided into provinces. The provinces, in turn, were divided into dioceses. The Church is still divided into dioceses and provinces. There is a bishop over each diocese. A number of dioceses form a province. The chief bishop in a province is known as an archbishop.

Check Your Knowledge

1. What changes came about for Catholics after the Edict of Milan was issued?
2. How did Constantine help the Church?
3. What did the bishops declare at the Council of Nicaea?
4. When is the Nicene Creed read today?
5. Who were the Doctors of the Church?

6. Who were the four Doctors from the eastern part of the empire?

7. Who were the four Doctors from the western part of the empire?

8. How was Augustine converted to Christianity?

9. How did Theodosius help the Church?

I0. What three ideas did the Church borrow from the Roman Empire?

I0. What three ideas did the Church borrow from the Roman Empire?

The Roman Empire Comes to an End

Constantine rules from Constantinople. The emperor Constantine is remembered principally for two things. We already know what one of these things is: He ended the persecution of the Church.

Constantine is also remembered because he decided not to rule from Rome. He moved to the city of Byzantium, at the eastern end of Europe, near Asia. Byzantium had been founded many centuries before as a Greek colony. Then it became a Greek city-state. When Constantine moved to Byzantium, the city had been in the Roman Empire for more than 400 years, but it was more Greek than Roman.

In Byzantium, Constantine built a great new palace for himself. He also erected many government buildings and many churches. He changed the name of the city to Constantinople, which means "Constantine's City."

Rome had ruled the world for about four hundred years. Now,

the world was to be ruled from Constantinople. Rome was never to be so powerful again.

Later, the empire was divided into two parts. The Eastern Empire was ruled from Constantinople. The Western Empire was ruled not from Rome but from Ravenna. There were now two Roman Empires, but Rome was not the capital of either one.

The Western Empire becomes weaker. The Roman Empire was probably becoming weaker even before Our Lord was born. Despite the fact that it was becoming weaker, the Roman Empire ruled the world for almost 500 years after the birth of Our Lord. Why was it able to do this? Because there was no strong enemy to conquer it. Almost all the countries in the world were part of the empire.

In time, however, the Western Empire became so weak that it came to an end. Sometimes we hear that the empire was conquered by "barbarians" from the north. It is true that many people from the north moved into the empire. They began to rule various parts of the empire. We will read about these people next. If the empire had been strong, however, these people could not have overcome it.

Who were the people who moved into the Western Empire? To the north of the Western Empire were many tribes whom the Romans had never been able to conquer. The Romans built forts along the border to protect the empire from these people. It was these people who were to become the rulers of Western Europe. They were to take the place of the Romans.

What shall we call these people? The Romans called them barbarians, which meant "strangers." When we call somebody a barbarian today, however, we usually mean he is at least half savage. Some of the people in northern Europe were barbarians in this sense. Others, however, were quite civilized.

Sometimes these people are called Teutons, or Germans. Perhaps that is a better name for them. When we call them Germans, however, you must not think that they were the same as the people who live in Germany today. It is true that the Germans of today are descendants of this race. But people in many other parts of Western Europe are descendants of this race, also. The Teutons moved into every part of the Western Empire.

German tribes lived in the forests of Northern Europe. They lived in houses made of rough logs. They wore the skins of wild animals. The men were tall and strong and handsome. They carried spears and shields, and they loved to fight. While the men were at war, the women took care of the homes, the fields, and the cattle.

The Germans who lived in the forests did not know about the One True God. They worshiped the sun, the moon, fire, and many other things. We get the names of the days of the week from the German gods and goddesses. Sunday is the sun's day. Monday is the moon's day. Wednesday is named for Woden, the chief god. Thursday is named for Thor, the god of thunder. Some of the Germans who lived close to the empire had become civilized. They lived much as the Romans did.

Not all the people who moved into the Western Empire were Germans. There were also Slavs and members of other races. There were even people from Asia. However, most of the people were probably Germans.

The Germans begin coming into the empire. The first Germans who came into the empire did so in a peaceful manner. The Romans did not have enough young men for their armies. Therefore, they invited young Germans to join the Roman army. These young men often brought their families with them. Soon there were many Germans in the empire. Some of the Germans became officers in the Roman army. Some even became generals. When other Germans wished to cross the border into the empire, these officers did not try very hard to stop them. The number of Germans in the Western Empire grew larger all the time.

Rome is captured by Germans. In the fourth century a fierce race called the Huns came out of central Asia into northern Europe. The Huns were the most terrible invaders Europe had ever seen. When they rode into battle they carried the heads of their enemies on their lances, as if to tell their foes what would happen to them.

The Huns were so fierce that even the Germans were afraid of them. More Germans swarmed over the borders in to the empire.

The Romans, too, were afraid of the Huns. The Emperor Valens told a group of Germans who were called Visigoths that they could come into the empire. Valens told the Visigoths, or West Goths, that he would supply them with food if they would help defend the empire against the Huns. The Visigoths no longer believed in the German gods, but they were not Catholics. They were Arians. This means they believed the heresy that had been started by Arius.

After they were in the empire for some time, the Visigoths did not think they were being treated justly. They began to fight the Romans. The Emperor Valens was killed in a battle with the Visigoths at Adrianople in 378 A.D. This was another turning point in history because a German force was able to defeat a Roman army in battle on Roman soil. This battle also marks the beginning of the conquest of the Western Empire by the Germans.

For a time there was peace between the Visigoths and the Romans. Then the Visigoths went to war again. This time they marched into Italy. In 410 A.D., under the leadership of Alaric, they captured the city of Rome.

The whole world was shocked when it learned that Rome had been captured" by the Visigoths. No one had been able to capture the city in more than 800 years. Even the great general Hannibal, of Carthage, had not been able to capture it. The people of Rome had been so proud of their city that they called it the "Eternal City." They thought it would last forever. Now it was in danger of being destroyed by the Visigoths.

People who were still pagans said, "As long as Rome was a pagan city, nobody could capture it. Rome became weak when the people became Christians."

Saint Augustine heard these arguments. That is one reason why he wrote the City of God. Saint Augustine said that no man-made city would last forever, no matter how great it seemed. The only city that will last forever is the City of God. The Catholic Church is the City of God.

The Germans spread over the empire. The Visigoths made peace with the Roman emperor. They left Italy and went into southern France and into Spain. Here they settled down. Both France and Spain were Roman provinces. The King of the Visigoths said that he was loyal to the Roman emperor. Actually, he did as he pleased, and the emperor had no control over the new kingdom of the Visigoths.

Germans who were called Vandals had moved into Spain before the Visigoths. The Visigoths got the better of the Vandals who moved on to North Africa. They captured most of North Africa and started a kingdom there. Saint Augustine died while the Vandals were besieging the city of Hippo in North Africa. The Vandals ruled the western end of the Mediterranean Sea. Ships from other countries were in danger of being captured by Vandal ships. In 455 A.D. the Vandals crossed into Italy and captured Rome. This was the second time the city had been captured in forty-five years. Sad times had come to the city that had once ruled the world. After stealing the treasures of the city and destroying everything in their way, the Vandals went back to Africa. Today, when someone willfully destroys something of value, we call him a vandal.

Everywhere German tribes were on the move. The Franks captured northern Gaul, which became known as the country of the Franks, or France. The Ostrogoths moved into southern Italy. The Lombards went into northern Italy. That section is still called Lombardy. Angles and Saxons and Jutes took over Britain. In most places the Roman army was too weak to stop the Germans. Instead of fighting Romans, the various German tribes often fought each other.

Pope Leo I saves Rome from the Huns. It was fear of the Huns that had brought many Germans into the empire. Shortly after the Vandals had captured Rome, the Huns began moving through Italy. The emperor fled from Ravenna. The people of Rome were terrified. They feared their city would be captured for the third time, and this time by the fierce Huns.

Pope Leo I went to meet Attila, the leader of the Huns who was called the "Scourge of God." After talking with the Pope, Attila made peace. Rome was saved. Attila died soon after, and his followers settled down in peace.

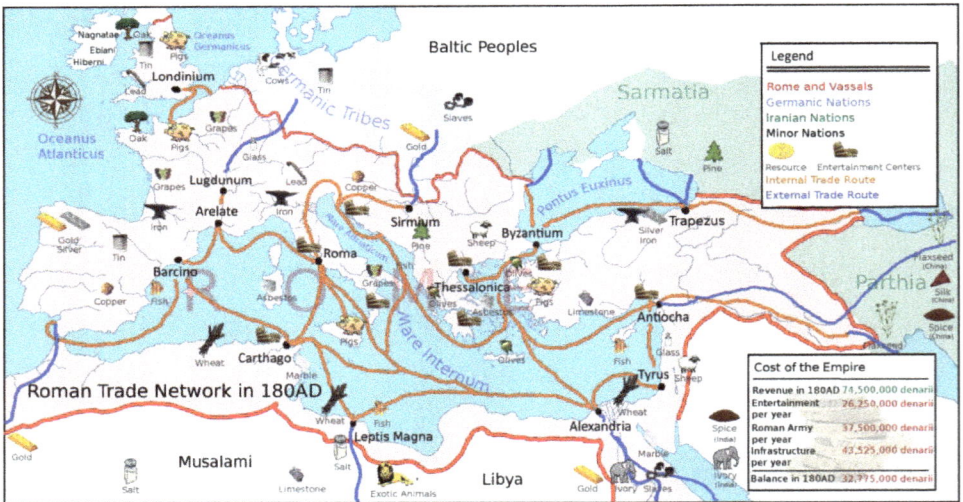

Roman Trade Network in 180AD

The Western Empire comes to an end. The power of the proud old Roman Empire was almost gone. North Africa and most of Western Europe were ruled by German kings who paid little or no attention to the emperor. In Italy itself most of the generals were Germans. These generals were more powerful than the emperor. In 476 A.D. a German general named

Odoacer removed the emperor from the throne. Odoacer made himself the king of Italy. Sometimes we say that the year 476 A.D. marks the end of the Western Empire. Actually, as we have seen, the empire had lost most of its power long before this. Still, 476 A.D. is a convenient date to remember.

Odoacer said that he was loyal to the Eastern emperor in faraway Constantinople. Actually, he ruled as he pleased, and so did his successors.

The Eastern Empire was still in existence. Thus, we might say that part of the old Roman Empire still remained. The Eastern Empire, however, had always been more Greek than Roman. As far as Western Europe was concerned, the Roman Empire had come to an end, although the name continued to be used.

Check Your Knowledge

1. From what city did Constantine rule the Roman Empire?
2. What caused the Roman Empire to become weak?
3. Into what parts of the Roman Empire did the Germans move?
4. Where do we get our names for the days of the week?
5. How did the Germans first get into the Roman Empire?
6. Who were the first to capture the city of Rome? ,
7. What was the importance of the battle at Adrianople?
8. Where did the Visigoths settle?
9. What three tribes conquered Britain?
10. Why do we say that the Western Empire ended in 476 A.D.?

The Church Faces New Problems After the Fall of the Empire

What would happen to Western Europe? It is hard to imagine the great change in Western Europe after the fall of the Western Empire. The empire had brought the Roman Peace to Western Europe. The empire had brought big cities and paved roads. It had brought beauty and learning. It had brought law and order.

Now all that was swept away. There was no longer any peace. After the various German tribes defeated the Romans, they began fighting each other. In the fighting, many cities and buildings and bridges were destroyed. Most of the Germans who moved into the empire did not know how to read or write. They did not appreciate the beautiful statues and buildings left by the Romans. They knew nothing about the system of laws the Romans had drawn up. For a time, it looked as though civilization might come to an end in Western Europe.

Perhaps you have heard people talk about the "dark ages." That name is sometimes given to the centuries after the fall of the Roman Empire, because many people were very ignorant. These people were ignorant largely because so many places of learning had been destroyed. Actually, these centuries were not as dark as some people say, and the name "dark ages" needs explanation. This term was used by men who did not know history, and it was made popular by some who were enemies of the Church. It is a very inexact term and should not be used. We shall see later that it was through the efforts of the monks that the learning of the ancient peoples was kept alive.

The Church undertook two great tasks. The Roman Empire

was gone, but the Catholic Church remained. Some enemies of the Church thought that the Church would die, too, now that the empire was gone. These people knew that Our Lord had lived and died in the Roman Empire, and that His Church had grown in the empire. They thought that the Church could not live without the empire. These people did not know that Our Lord had promised that He would be with His Church until the end of time. The Church had lived through the days when the Roman emperors had persecuted it. The Church would continue to live now that the empire was gone. Although the Church faced grave problems, there was no doubt that they would be solved.

The two greatest tasks which the Church undertook in Western Europe were perhaps these:

I. It must convert the Germans who had overrun Europe. Some of these Germans were pagans who still worshiped their false gods. Some were heretics who hated the Catholic religion. Very few were Catholics.

2. It must save what was good in Roman civilization.

The Church had been weakened. The Church did not seem very strong when it began these two great tasks. The Pope still lived in Rome, but that city was now largely in ruins. Many bishops and priests had been killed. Many churches had been destroyed. The Pope found it difficult to get in touch with the priests and bishops who were left. Some lived in lands where the rulers did not like the Catholic religion. Others lived in places that were hard to reach because so many Roman roads had been destroyed.

There were many Catholics scattered over Western Europe. They had been converted before the empire came to an end. Most of these Catholics had no priests. They could not attend Mass or receive the sacraments. Without priests the people were in danger of losing their Faith.

The picture was not entirely black, however. There were three bright spots. These were the Eastern Empire, Ireland, and the kingdom of the Franks.

The Eastern Empire was still Catholic. The Germans who overran Western Europe did not conquer the Eastern Empire. This remained a Christian region and a civilized area. Throughout the Eastern Empire there were magnificent churches, amphitheaters, schools, libraries, and paved roads. Merchants came to Constantinople to buy and sell silks, rugs, spices, and many other things.

The great Emperor Justinian came· to the throne in 527. Justinian even won back Italy and part of North Africa. Justinian's greatest work was to gather together all the laws of the Roman Empire. This was called Justinian's Code. The Romans were noted for their laws, and Justinian saved them for us. Many of our laws today are influenced by Justinian's Code.

When the Pope needed missionaries for Western Europe, he was able to get many of them from the Eastern Empire.

Ireland remains a Catholic country. Back in the days of the Roman Empire, a young Roman citizen named Patrick was kidnaped. This was around the year 400 A.D. Patrick was taken to Ireland. There he was sold as a slave. For six years Patrick tended the flocks for his master. He loved the Irish people and he learned to speak their language. Patrick was a Catholic. He longed to teach the Irish people about God.

Patrick escaped from Ireland. For many years he studied and prepared to be a missionary. He became a priest and a bishop. Then he went back to his beloved Ireland. Before he died he had succeeded in bringing nearly all the Irish people into the Church. Ireland has been a strong Catholic country ever since.

Ireland was one country of Western Europe which was not overrun by the Germans. Churches continued to stand. People continued to go to Mass and receive the sacraments. Young men continued to study for the priesthood. There were few schools left on the continent of Europe, but the Irish monas -teries had many good schools. Scholars from all over Europe came to Ireland. The country became known as the "Isle of Saints and Scholars."

After the fall of the empire, missionaries from Ireland went forth to convert the people in all parts of Western Europe. **The Franks become Catholics**. Along the Rhine River lived a group of German tribes who were called Franks. Five years after the last emperor of the West had been put off the throne, a fifteen year old boy became king of one of these tribes. The boy's name was Clovis. In time Clovis united all the tribes of Franks under his rule. He became the king of the Franks.

Clovis next conquered most of Gaul, or what is now France. Gaul had been conquered by Julius Caesar four centuries earlier. It had been part of the Roman Empire. The people spoke Latin, and most of them were Catholics. Clovis was kind and just to the people of Gaul. He did not treat them as conquered people. He made them the equals of his own Franks. He allowed them to practice Catholicism. Clovis' wife Clotilda was a Catholic. One day Clovis was in danger of losing an important battle. He promised that if he won the battle he, too, would become a Catholic. He did win, and he kept his promise. He and 3000 of his followers were baptized on Christmas Day in 496 A.D.

The kingdom ruled by Clovis continued to grow. It included France, the Netherlands, Switzerland, and a large part of Germany.

Clovis brought law and order and peace to his region. He welcomed priests and bishops. He helped build churches. To some extent, the kingdom of the Franks had taken the place of the old Western Empire.

Because of the support received in the kingdom of the Franks, the Church was better able to bring the word of Christ to all Western Europe.

Check Your Knowledge

1. What had the Roman Empire brought to Western Europe?
2. What were the two greatest problems faced by the Church after the fall of the empire?
3. Why were many Catholics in Europe in danger of losing their Faith?
4. From where was the Pope able to get many missionaries?
5. How did Saint Patrick first meet the Irish people?
6. What were the three "bright spots" for the Church after the

empire fell?

7. Where did the Franks live at first?

8. What place in Western Europe continued to have fine schools?

9. What land did the Franks conquer?

10. How did Clovis treat the conquered Gauls?

CPSIA information can be obtained
at www.ICGtesting.com
Printed in the USA
BVHW021421150922
647140BV00013B/354

9 781087 881492